professionalizing
motherhood

Praise for *Professionalizing Motherhood* by Jill Savage

Jill's heart and her ability to communicate the principles in *Professionalizing Motherhood* profoundly touched my heart. In her simplistic yet practical way she presents hope for today's mothers in their search for significance and their importance in being moms.

Elise Arndt
author of *A Mother's Touch*
and *A Mother's Time*

A practical, honest, and inspiring manifesto for the most powerful person on earth—mother. In a culture hostile to full-time mothering, Jill Savage reframes a woman's decision to rear her children herself. She presents a compelling new way of looking at motherhood—as a fulfilling profession—and challenges mothers everywhere to view child-rearing as a career worthy of their time, talents, and wholehearted commitment. A needed book!

Brenda M. Hunter, Ph.D.
author of *Home by Choice*
and *The Power of Mother Love*

Finally! A book that shows you why motherhood is a High Professional Calling! Jill's delightful humor and practical tips will equip you for each challenge you face in raising kids. In the process you'll know and feel that your job is truly significant.

Susan Alexander Yates
author of *And Then I Had Kids*
and *Encouragement for Mothers of Young Children*

Professionalizing Motherhood

Encouraging, Educating, and Equipping Mothers at Home

Jill Savage

Founder and Director of Hearts at Home

ZONDERVAN™

GRAND RAPIDS, MICHIGAN 49530

We want to hear from you. Please send your comments about this book to us in care of the address below. Thank you.

GRAND RAPIDS, MICHIGAN 49530

www.zondervan.com

ZONDERVAN™

Professionalizing Motherhood
Copyright © 2001 by Jill Savage

Requests for information should be addressed to:
Zondervan, *Grand Rapids, Michigan 49530*

Library of Congress Cataloging-in-Publication Data
Savage, Jill, 1964–
    Professionalizing motherhood : encouraging, educating, and equipping mothers at home / Jill Savage.
       p.   cm.
    Includes bibliographical references.
    ISBN 0-310-23741-6 (pbk.)
    1. Mothers.   2. Homemakers.   3. Family.   4. Motherhood—Religious aspects—Christianity.   I. Title.
HQ759 .S267 2001
306.874'3—dc21
                                                    2001017678

Published in association with Yates & Yates, LLP, Literary Agent, Orange, CA.

Interior design by Melissa Elenbaas

Printed in the United States of America

01 02 03 04 05 06 /❖ DC/ 10 9 8 7 6 5 4 3 2

CONTENTS

Acknowledgments   7

Introduction   9

PART 1 — SHIFT YOUR THINKING

1. Professionalizing Motherhood   15
2. So What Did You Do Today?   27
3. Take Care of the Caregiver   40

PART 2 — DETERMINE YOUR STRATEGY

4. Do You Know Your True Value?   59
5. Is Your Family Marriage-Centered?   70
6. Where Are My Coworkers?   80

PART 3 — TOOLS OF THE TRADE

7. Fun: You've Got to Have a Good Time!   93
8. Prayer: An Indispensable Tool   106
9. Creativity: Let the Creative Juices Flow!   122
10. Grace: It Has a Place in Your Home   137
11. Humor: Let's Laugh a Bit!   152
12. Organization: I Can't Go Anywhere Without My Planner!   163

PART 4 — ESTABLISH YOUR CAREER TRAINING AND DEVELOPMENT

13. Develop Your Partnership with God   173
14. Parent with Purpose   183
15. Make Your House a Home   199

16. Build an Incredible Resumé!   211

Appendix A: A Message for the Husband of a
Woman in the Profession of Motherhood   216

Appendix B: My Professional Goals   219

Appendix C: Professional Resources for Mothers
at Home   221

ACKNOWLEDGMENTS

WITH SPECIAL THANKS:

To all of the Hearts at Home staff. You are my friends and co-laborers in ministry. Thank you for your commitment to the profession of motherhood and thank you for the encouragement you gave me during this project.

To my friends and family who pored over manuscripts: Mike and Becky, Holly, Doris, Cathy, Tammy, Julie, Jennifer, Sherri, Juli, and Mark. Your input and honesty helped me greatly.

To Larry and Laurie, who let me use their cabin as a writing getaway. Thank you for sharing your beautiful home with me.

To my friends Shawn, Tammy, Irene, Julie, Cathy, and Doris who helped with kids, carpooling, and anything else that needed to be done in the midst of book deadlines. Thank you to all my dear friends—I can't possibly name them all—who prayed, encouraged, and helped me in a variety of ways.

To my prayer team: Elise, Charlene, Dave, and Jennifer; and those in my small group: Julie, Cathy, Rita, Tammy, Shawn, Lora, and Dawn. Thank you for spending time on your knees for me.

To my dear friend and co-laborer in ministry, Paul Meyer. You believed in me as a woman in ministry leadership even before I believed in myself.

To Cindy Hays and Sue Brower of Zondervan for catching the vision of Hearts at Home and helping to make this project a reality!

To Sealy and Susan Yates, my literary agents. Thank you, first, for believing in the ministry of Hearts at Home. Your help in making published resources available to mothers at home across the world means so much to me.

To my sister-in-law, Denise. Thank you for your words of encouragement and for reading chapters for me.

To my sisters, Jackie and Juli. Thank you for your encouragement. Now that this project is finished, I believe it's time to celebrate with some Jello Cheesecake!

To my parents, Duane and Patsy Fleener, and my grandma, Annabelle Chambers. Thank you for your incredible support over the years. Dad, thank you for insisting on good grammar and giving me encouragement in my speaking and writing from the time I won my first speech contest and published my first article to the present. Mom, thank you for modeling for me the importance of the profession of motherhood. I love you!

To my children, Anne, Evan, Erica, and Austin, who allow me to enjoy the profession of motherhood to the fullest.

To my dear husband, Mark, who is my teammate, my confidante, my best friend. Thank you for supporting me in this ministry adventure. Thank you for serving as cook, secretary, taxi driver, and proofreader extraordinaire! I love you!

To Jesus Christ, my Lord and Savior, for loving me, saving me, and equipping me. Thank you, Lord, for your words, your Truth, and your direction both in the ministry of Hearts at Home and during this writing project.

INTRODUCTION

I AM CERTAIN THAT THE ORIGINS OF THIS BOOK, AND OF THE MINISTRY OF Hearts at Home, which has now touched the lives of over forty thousand women, will not be lost on you. In fact, I'm hoping you'll identify with them completely. Perhaps the same thing that motivated you to pick up this book is the very thing that set me on the surprising course I am now traveling.

The origins of it all lay quite simply in my realizing that this "mom" thing, once I got into it, was a lot harder, a lot bigger, and a lot more challenging than I felt equipped to handle. Let me fill you in on what I mean.

In May of 1989, I asked eight women to join me each Wednesday morning to encourage one another in homemaking. Having no extended family nearby, I had a strong desire to know more about my role as wife, mother, and homemaker. I knew I could learn a lot from other women and desired regular interaction to facilitate growth. The feeling was mutual among the other women, too. They were all mothers of young children and wanted a mixture of friendship, encouragement, and education.

We began meeting regularly. We hired one sitter to watch our children in the basement while we met upstairs in my living room. We discussed books we were reading, shared parenting tips, challenged one another in our marriages, and learned homemaking ideas from one another. Before we knew it there weren't just eight of us anymore. As we met other women at the McDonald's Playland or at story hour at the library, we invited them to join us at our moms' group. Before long we needed more than one sitter and we were quickly outgrowing my living room.

Several years later we formalized our moms' group, giving it the name "Mom2Mom" and moving it to a local church facility. That group is still meeting today, more than ten years later, with about 150 women in attendance each week and over 200 children in the "Kid2Kid" program.

In 1993, when Mom2Mom was experiencing exponential growth, God placed on my heart the need to encourage mothers outside of our community. "After all, if there was this much need in our little community, what kind of need is there outside of our area?" I asked myself.

My background is in music education. During my college years, the music staff at Butler University in Indianapolis encouraged us to belong to professional organizations. Each of those organizations held an annual conference. Those events energized me so I always came back full of vision for my role as a music teacher, equipped with many new ideas that I could hardly wait to try in the classroom, and excited about my career choice.

As I found myself in motherhood for the long haul, I began to think back on those conferences that I had attended years ago. I remembered the renewed vision they had given me. And I began to think that I needed such an event for my new career: motherhood. Growing numbers at our moms' group fueled that vision. I asked several women from Mom2Mom to join me in praying about a conference for moms.

Nine months later we hosted our first Hearts at Home conference. Expecting approximately five hundred women to attend, marketing efforts were focused within a three-hour radius of Bloomington, Illinois. We were overwhelmed, though, when 1,100 women from ten states registered for that conference! God knew the need that was out there. Through this, God showed us the importance of listening to Him and following His lead.

In the years since that first event in 1994, Hearts at Home has grown to be an organization committed to the career of motherhood. In a world where stay-at-home motherhood is seen as a disposable role, we believe it is a valid profession. The Hearts at Home organization offers a wide variety of resources in addition to its annual conferences. We are a nondenominational professional organization for mothers at home or those who want to be at home. Our desire is to exalt God while educating and encouraging women in their personal and family lives.

Hearts at Home is managed by a unique group of women, almost all mothers at home. Over 150 moms (and several dads!) blend their talents and gifts to minister to the needs of women in the profession of motherhood. It has been wonderful to see God provide for the volunteer needs of this growing organization.

At the same time, because we are all mothers at home, we must balance the growth of our organization with continuing to do our best for our own families. Our desire would be to have a Hearts at Home conference in every state. Someday God may provide for this, but for now we have set our sites on several regional events each year in addition to growing our resources for women in the profession of motherhood.

One result of my desire to educate, encourage, and equip mothers at home to be all they can be is the book you are now holding in your hands. This book is designed to bring the message of Hearts at Home into the life of any woman who picks it up. That message is the incredible value of motherhood. It is about taking advantage of a season of life that will never be given back to you. It is about keeping your heart at home. It is about professionalizing motherhood.

Whether or not you've ever considered motherhood a valid profession, I hope you'll be encouraged and challenged by the message of this book to shift your thinking, determine your strategy, know the tools of your trade, and establish your career training and development. Join me in the journey of exploring one of the most rewarding occupations available to women: the profession of motherhood.

part *1*

SHIFT YOUR THINKING

chapter 1

PROFESSIONALIZING MOTHERHOOD

So what do you do?" That is certainly the question of the day, isn't it? It's also a question that makes some of us who stay home cringe when it is posed to us. We don't know how to answer it. Some of us choose to be creative with a response such as, "I'm currently researching the development of children." And yet others of us respond with, "Oh, I'm *just* a mom."

Aren't both of those responses telling? The first type of response indicates that the terms *wife* and *mother* are not important enough. They alone do not indicate a "real profession." By using a creative title we hope we will be respected more, valued for our knowledge in some area, and interesting enough for continued conversation. I've talked to far too many women who have attended social gatherings with their husbands or former coworkers only to find that when they mention they are "a stay-at-home mom," the conversation seems to come to a halt. It is as if the other person determines that you can't possibly have much to offer to the conversation because you are not "educated enough" or "sharp enough" to contribute . . . after all, you are "only" a mom—how hard can that be?

Conversely, with the second response, we ourselves are suggesting that we are "second class." The word *just* implies that our responsibilities are somehow inferior to those of other people. Because we receive no monetary compensation for our position, we begin to buy into the lie that we are not contributing as we should. We are indeed "just moms."

I believe it is time for a new response. I believe we need to remove the "just" from our response. We need to stand up straight, offer no apology for what we do, and respond with, "I am a wife and a mother, and I love my job!" With great pride in our chosen career, we must share with people that we are in the "profession of motherhood."

A CHANGE OF PLANS

I found myself in full-time motherhood by accident. It did not begin as an intentional career choice for me. I was a teacher, living in Indianapolis, Indiana. Actually, I had just finished my teaching degree when my husband, Mark, decided to change careers. Mark felt God calling him to the ministry, so we packed up our little family and moved to Lincoln, Illinois. Anne was a two-year-old at the time and Evan was ten weeks old. To become an ordained minister, Mark had four years of full-time school ahead of him.

Our perfect plan for our new life included my finding a teaching job, Mark's caring for the kids when he was not in class, and a sitter's providing daycare for the majority of the daytime hours. We were not prepared, however, for the possibility of a lack of teaching jobs in the area. I interviewed at several schools, but found nothing available. With two children at home, we determined that most hourly paying jobs would not be worth my time since the take-home pay would just barely cover our childcare expenses.

Because we lived in a married student housing unit, we decided to put Plan B into action: I would provide daycare in our home. There were many other students who also needed daycare, and I could offer that service for those families. We would have a steady income and our children wouldn't need childcare. It seemed like the logical option. This plan worked for our family during the first year and a half of Mark's schooling.

Those eighteen months were indeed a time of growth. We couldn't afford anything but the bare minimum in health insurance. We had very little money for food. As I reflect on that time, I still don't know how we ever paid our bills on about $6,000 a year. But we did, because God took care of our every need. When grocery money ran out, we'd find groceries on our doorstep. When we didn't have enough to pay bills, we would receive an unexpected check in the mail. When we needed clothes for the kids, someone would give us just what we needed. It was an incredible lesson in God's faithfulness.

The most important lesson He taught me, however, came from caring for those children. I began to see the other side of leaving children in someone else's care. The children received excellent care in my home, but when they fell down, they didn't want me—they wanted Mommy. When their feelings got hurt, they didn't want me—they wanted Mommy. When they were coming down with a cold or weren't feeling well, they didn't want me—they wanted Mommy.

Furthermore, I cared for a few grade school children after school. When they arrived at my home, they were bubbling over with excitement. They told me about their day. They shared with me about their friends. They showed me their papers and their craft projects because it was fresh on their minds and they were so proud. By the time Mom or Dad picked them up, that information was no longer pertinent. They were tired and ready to go home, eat dinner, and go to bed. For some of those families, I could communicate what the child had told me, but I could not adequately share the pride and enthusiasm I had seen earlier in the day.

What an eye-opening experience that was for me! I had never once considered what I might be missing when leaving my children in someone else's care or how the children might be affected. I certainly had never thought about how short the season of children at home really is in a family's life. My eyes were opened, and my heart for my children and my home was beginning to grow.

THE VALUE OF OUR CHILDREN

We keep hearing the questions asked, "What is happening to the children of today? Why do we have such violence? Why are children killing? Why is there such a lack of respect among the youth of this generation?" Although there are several contributing factors to this situation, I believe our society's lack of value for children is chiefly to blame.

We have given careers, money, and gadgets a higher value than our children. We have allowed our minds to be influenced by the media's message that "being home" is something of the past. We have bought into the lie that staying home to raise our children is a waste of our minds. Therefore, we have valued our jobs and our education more than our children.

When Anne, our firstborn, was small, I continued my education and left her in several different home daycare situations. I kept looking for the "best" childcare for her. What mother wouldn't? Initially I looked for someone to come to our home. I valued Anne's being in our own home where things were familiar to her.

But through it all I did not realize what was really best for Anne. In my quest to find the right caregiver, I did not consider myself as a candidate. Furthermore, I was missing her inherent value as a growing person who needed to be taught all about the world around her. Her value as a future member of the adult community and the impact she could have on the world around her escaped me. I did not understand that she needed a strong family identity to help her know who she was and what she stood for in an ever-changing world. Most important, I did not consider the fact that God had given her to *me* to teach her about her worth and value in Christ.

I was also clueless about just how much time and energy it takes to raise a family!

When we have a goal of raising morally conscious, emotionally stable, and relationally strong children, we can't help but see the time and energy it will take. But when we realize our children are gifts from God, entrusted to our care, we see them as much more than just obligations added to our busy schedules.

My years of home daycare opened my eyes to the needs of children. For the first time in my life, I began to value my children for the gifts they are and I began to consider seriously the responsibility of raising them. My thinking changed from "Who is best suited to care for them?" to "I am their mother and they deserve my best."

THE VALUE OF THE HOME

As God was growing my heart for my children, He was also growing my heart for my home. I truly had not given much thought to the atmosphere of my home. I certainly "kept house" (although at times I didn't do that very well!), but I had not known the difference between homemaking and housekeeping.

As God was changing my heart, He instilled in me a desire to do more than "keep house." He gave me the desire to "make a home."

Holly Schurter, a mother of eight, puts it so well in a letter she wrote to her grown daughter who was soon to become a mother for the first time:

> Cultivate the skills, not only of housekeeping, but of making a home for your family. As you know already, they are not always exactly the same.
>
> Housekeeping consists of the laundry, the dishes, the toilets, and floors that need to be scrubbed, but homemaking is something else. The difference between housekeeping and homemaking is the difference between a barren field and a lovely, fragrant garden.
>
> Homemaking is the deliberate cultivation of beauty and productivity in family relationships. Homemaking is about helping your family feel loved and comforted. Homemaking is about celebrating each other, and about caring for each other, as well as for your friends and extended families and even the occasional stranger. Anyone can keep house. Not everyone bothers to make a home.

When you combine the responsibilities of preparing children for adulthood and cultivating a warm home, you have a full-time job ahead of you.

DON'T WE NEED TWO INCOMES?

Today's parents are heavily influenced by the media. We have so much information and so many opinions thrown our way we become easily confused by the difference between what is true and what is a lie. It all gets very confusing.

Does it take two incomes for a family to survive today? We hear the message that if you want to give your kid what he "needs," you will have to have two incomes. Is it true that the cost of housing, schooling, and taxes eat up so much of the family's income, you need additional monies coming in to cover the rest of the living expenses? Are you aware that over 7.7 million[1] families in the United States live on one income? For many of these families it is not a luxury but a sacrifice they are willing to make. The husband is not making more than an average salary, and they are living in average homes. They accomplish this in many ways, including being thrifty with clothes buying, grocery shopping with a carefully planned budget, and keeping a comfortable home without falling prey to every fad that comes along. The bottom line is that many of these families are living happily with less than what we are told by media that we *need*.

Bill Flick, a newspaper columnist for *The Pantagraph* in Illinois, questions the concept of the "high cost of living." He says it's more like "the high cost of the way we choose to live." The desire to "keep up with the Joneses" affects us whether we realize it or not. We start to believe we need certain things for the basic existence of daily life. Mark and I have been trying to think through our purchases with this in mind. We ask ourselves, "Do we really need this or do we just want it?" One area we have found to cut costs is cable television. Yes, you *can* get TV reception without cable—even in rural areas! We're living proof of that. We haven't had cable television for fourteen years. Our children have not been hurt by the absence of cable in our home. Are there times we wish we had cable? Yes, there are. Can we afford it? No, it doesn't fit into our budget. So we use an antenna and watch the basic network channels.

It *is* possible to live on one income in today's society, but it takes some willingness to practice delayed gratification. Delaying some of the things we would like to have now in exchange for doing something we need to do now is what it is all about. As much as I'd like to have a new car (for once in my life!) or new furniture in just one room of our home, I choose to be happy without those things in order to be home with my children. It's a concept we don't hear much about today, but it's one we can learn to embrace. By practicing delayed gratification we are on our way to understanding what's really important in life—people, not things. The choices we make now will affect our families' lives and future. One day when we reflect on the memories, will they be positive or negative?

As a mother, am I making the choices I need to make now in order to live without regrets in the future?

A CHANGE IN CAREERS

After my experience of providing daycare in my home full time for a little over a year, my husband started an internship in Bloomington, Illinois, which required that he commute about sixty miles round trip to school each day. So, we moved to Bloomington, a city where we knew no one. Looking back, this move made absolutely no sense: We doubled our rent and lost the daycare income. The sense of direction God had given us to make this move, however, could not be ignored. We had to walk through the door God had opened. We did, and once again, He provided.

This move was different from the last one, though. This time we were fully committed to my being home with our children. My heart had been changed. Mark's heart had been changed, too, as he realized the value of my full-time commitment to our family. Our financial circumstances hadn't changed, though. In fact, they were becoming worse. What were we going to do?

As we wondered what God's plan was for us, He affirmed the commitments we had for our family. I provided care for one other child in my home, rather than for a house full of children. I also put my music skills to work teaching piano and voice in our home several evenings a week. Mark took on odd jobs as his schooling schedule would allow ... *and we made it*. Many times God interceded and provided in supernatural ways. The experience grew our faith at an incredible rate.

At that time, I told myself I would be home while the children were small. When they went to school, I planned to seek a teaching position. As Anne entered kindergarten, however, we found ourselves expecting a new member in our family. When Erica was born, Anne was six and Evan was four. I knew then that I would be home for at least another six years.

During those years I developed a close friendship with another woman whose youngest child was born just four weeks after Erica. We spent much time together and enjoyed encouraging one another in homemaking. At the same time, the small moms' group that I had started in my home when we moved to Bloomington was growing. The new friendships made those baby and toddler years fly by so quickly.

As Erica began her last year of preschool, I began to anticipate a new season of life. Mark and I decided our family was complete. We made arrangements to make that a permanent decision. But, before Mark could make it in for the surgery, we discovered that we would be adding another little Savage to our family. Austin was born three days before Erica started kindergarten. I was beginning to feel as though I was going to be home with preschoolers for the rest of my life!

Now with a newborn (the others were eleven, nine, and six years old), I realized I would be home another five years, at least. I wasn't prepared, however, for what was happening as our older children were entering the preteen and teen years. Although I had focused on the physical needs of caring for small children, I was not prepared for the emotional needs my growing children would have, for the time and energy it would take to teach them about relationships and the world around them, and for how they would need me to help them cope with the emotional wounds that would come as they interacted in the world. Until then I had not understood that as they were coming closer and closer to adulthood, I would actually have more and more things to teach them. I had a huge job ahead of me leading and encouraging them as their world expanded and ushering them into adulthood.

God was once again changing my heart. For the first time in my life, I laid the career of teaching aside indefinitely and decided that raising my family *was* my career. It was God's plan for this season of my life. It was a job I needed to take seriously. I may very well teach school someday or I may not. What I do know is that, God willing, I will be home with my children until they reach adulthood.

Have I grieved the loss of a dream? You bet. Have I shed tears over not using my degree? Yes, I have. But if you ask me which I would regret more—missing the years my children are home or missing the years of teaching—without a doubt my answer would be missing the years my children are home. So as I look to their future, I have determined what I need to do now.

Do you realize the average mother has approximately twenty years to work outside the home *after* her children are grown? That means there will be plenty of years for me to teach if I choose to do so after my children are on their own. On the other hand, twenty years is all I have to nurture and teach my children—the first twenty years of their lives!

YOU'RE AT HOME AND YOUR CHILDREN ARE IN SCHOOL?

During one of our early Mom2Mom meetings, we asked Karen, an empty nest mother, to come and share her experience with our group. In preparation for her time spent with us, Karen asked her three grown children to express (in letter form) what it meant to them to have a mother at home. My children were all preschoolers at the time and her children's remarks have stayed with me to this day. One common thread ran through all three of the letters Karen read that day. All three children shared how important it had been to them that their mom was home for them during their teenage years! One shared that her mom's presence after school helped her sort through the challenges of teenage relationships. Another shared that her mom's availability to help with school functions and extracurricular activities meant so much to her. And her son felt that just knowing Mom was home and that he was accountable to her kept him out of trouble.

The epidemic of empty houses after school and during the summer only adds to the temptations teens face. Teenagers are not yet adults and they need direction and supervision. Dr. Brenda Hunter states in her book, *Home by Choice*,[2]

"Our children need our time, attention, and presence to grow well into themselves. They need someone at home who's passionately concerned about them, not just during the early years but also over the long haul."

MOTHERHOOD: A PROUD PROFESSION

When I started out on my career track in college, I knew I wanted to be a teacher. That was my goal. As far as I could see, teaching music was what I would do throughout my life. I think most of us start our adult lives with those kinds of dreams.

What I didn't understand was that it is perfectly okay to change careers. If I had gone from being a teacher to being a scientist, that would have been easily accepted and maybe even applauded. If I had taken my teaching skills and changed from teaching high school to teaching in some other form of higher education, it would have been considered very wise. But to decide to be a mom, full time? Well, then I'd be wasting my education. Isn't that the way we think? Isn't that the way some of our parents (who may have put us through college) think? Isn't that the message society proclaims so freely?

I'd like to suggest otherwise. I'd like to raise the value of motherhood to a higher level in everyone's mind. I'd like us to consider it a valid career choice. I'd like us to call it what it is—a profession. And I'd like those of us working as full-time mothers to think of ourselves as what we are—professionals. A woman who leaves the paid workforce to become a full-time mother is embarking on a positive and exciting lateral career move!

A career or profession is a job that we commit ourselves to for a season of time. Often it is an occupation we take so seriously that we have sought special training to become the best we can at it. When we think about the concept of a profession, we are identifying a job that we feel is important enough for our time and our energy. It is also a job that enriches our lives in some shape or form. The profession of motherhood certainly meets all of these definitions.

When God created Adam and Eve, He designed them to fulfill specific, complementary roles and responsibilities—roles that had equal value in His eyes. The design allows the husband and wife to build a family that works well together.

He designed man to be the provider. He made him task oriented. He gave him a strong body to perform manual labor and to defend his family.

When God designed woman, He created her to be relational. He gave her a strong nurturing sense. He designed her body to bear, nurse, and nurture children.

As a society, though, we've tried to debunk such old-fashioned ideas. After all, women are just as capable as men. Women should have equal opportunities. Yet in our quest for equal opportunities, we have forgotten an entire sector of the human race: our children. We have rushed to the front lines to fight for equality while failing to face our responsibility in raising the next generation.

To send children into adulthood who are morally responsible and emotionally mature takes an incredible amount of time and energy. It takes intelligence and skill. To run all the activities of a typical family requires an ability to manage resources of time, money, and energy. We must not devalue the responsibilities of caring for a family. We must take this job seriously. *The profession of motherhood is about devoting your good mind and exceptional skills to the nurturing of your family.*

Have you changed or are you considering changing the career direction of your life? Are you considering the career of motherhood? Have you ever considered *motherhood* to be a valid profession? I invite you to join this team of professional women who are committed to motherhood!

Identifying motherhood as a profession is the first step in setting the career direction of your life. The next step is redefining just what *accomplishment* is in the life of a mother. An adjustment in perspective, a redefinition of accomplishment, and a new kind of "to do" list are essential in making the transition successfully.

──────────── **A STEP FURTHER . . .** ────────────

How can your family practice delayed gratification in order to lessen the need for two incomes?

Identify any misconceptions you have had concerning the value of full-time motherhood. Can you identify the sources of those misconceptions (media, family members, coworkers, etc.)?

༄༅

Have you ever considered the needs of children in their teen years? Identify five reasons why teens need a parent at home.

chapter 2

So What Did You Do Today?

IT WAS A COLD DAY. ANNE HAD BEEN TO KINDERGARTEN THAT AFTERNOON, Evan was home all day, and Erica, who was two months old, had screamed seven out of the nine hours I had been awake.

Mark blew in the door with his usual after-work hugs for the kids, a kiss on the cheek for me, and that infamous question, "So what did you do today?" If I hadn't been holding a two-month-old baby, I'm sure I would have thrown something at him. Instead I succumbed to the tears that were just waiting to happen. I remember saying some garbled mess about not knowing exactly what I did today. Through my tears I told him I wasn't sure I was cut out for this job. I didn't know if I could handle much more. Needless to say, I was an emotional wreck.

Maybe you've been there; most of us have. This emotional state is a mixture of feeling overwhelmed, unequipped, and just plain old tired. Ultimately, though, it is often fueled by the underlying question, "What exactly am I accomplishing?"

Webster's Dictionary defines accomplishment as "something done successfully; work completed." Therein lies our problem. A woman in the profession of motherhood doesn't often see ultimate success for more than a dozen years, and the responsibilities of motherhood are such that we feel our work is *never* completed. Those initial thoughts, however, are quite deceiving. Let's look at the realities of motherhood and how we can find a new perspective on accomplishment.

CAN'T I FINISH ANYTHING?

When Anne and Evan were preschoolers I organized a moms' group that met weekly. As we were giving vision and form to our weekly meeting times, we all agreed on the need to include craft projects in our schedule. Now, let me tell you—I am what you would call "craft challenged." Creativity is certainly not one of my gifts. But despite my lack of creativity, even *I* was drawn to this idea, not because it was something I particularly enjoyed doing, but because I knew it would give me a sense of accomplishment.

Over the years, we created floral arrangements, decorated gift bags, and completed dozens of craft projects. We stenciled, painted, stamped, and glued. When planning the craft projects, we had only two guidelines: They had to be inexpensive (we were all living on one income), and they had to be completed within two hours. No uncompleted projects allowed. There could be no expectation of "taking it home to finish." Why? Because our goal for the craft projects was for us to feel a sense of accomplishment. Each time we looked at the finished product we could say, "I did that!" More important, we could say, "I did that, and it stayed done!"

Have you ever stopped to think about how much time you spend in the kitchen doing the same things over and over again? We start with breakfast, then it's a mid-morning snack, and lunch follows. Mid-afternoon brings about another snack, then it's dinner time, and many families add an evening or bedtime snack. No wonder I have dreams of being able to put a sign on the kitchen door that says, "Kitchen Closed."

We do the laundry and the clothes get dirty again. We clean the bathroom only to find toothpaste in the sink five minutes later. We change a diaper only to have it soiled within minutes. We wipe the sand off a toddler's clothes so he can come in the house to go potty, only to have him return outside to the sandbox. We wash the dishes and they are used again. We prepare food that is eaten in minutes and repeat the process a few hours later. The duties that make up our job simply do not stay finished. But despite the fact that our efforts never seem to produce anything that stays done, what we do *is* a necessary and essential part of life!

When we measure our sense of accomplishment against what the world deems as accomplishment, we are using the wrong measuring tool. *Raising children needs a different "measuring stick" to determine our level of accomplishment. We can't listen to the cries of our culture that say accomplishment comes from a paycheck, an award, or a position or title.* We can't buy into the belief that accomplishment is measured by something that stays finished. Success in the profession of motherhood comes from redefining our goals. It comes from changing our vision from short-term to long-term, and it comes from adjusting our concept of just what our "to do" lists should look like. It takes a change in perspective.

WE HAVE ONE PRIMARY GOAL

We assume accomplishment is indicated by tangible results. Most often we want those results to closely follow the efforts we have invested. We are a very accomplishment-oriented society. We measure people's worth by what they do, by what they achieve. This approach sets a very dangerous trap for mothers at home. If we don't stop and change our perspective, we will find ourselves in a never-ending state of frustration.

The profession of motherhood has one primary goal—to see a child grow into a mature, godly, respectful, and loving adult. This is a task that takes an investment of more than eighteen years for each child. And that is an incredibly *long* long-term goal! With a goal like that, we are not often going to see results that closely follow the effort we have put forth. We may be pursuing a result that we will only see decades from now, but let's not lose sight, over time, of our extremely important goal. Motherhood is vitally important and a worthy profession to commit ourselves to.

When you influence the life of a child, you mold and shape the next generation. When you invest in the next generation, you are making an impact on society. This is why the profession of motherhood is so very important! No profession will have a greater impact.

In my work with women, I often hear moms who are in the empty-nest season of life say, "I wish I'd spent more time with my children." As women in the child-rearing season of life, our time to make decisions that will determine whether we will look back on these years with satisfaction or with regret is now. Leading a child through childhood is too important a job to coast through without a plan and then look back upon with regret. I *need* to be a professional in how I go about this job of being a mom.

As we set our goal of shepherding our children through childhood into adolescence and ultimately into adulthood, our job is to help them make the transition from our values and teachings to their own beliefs and values. When they are four we teach them how to share what they have in hopes that when they are fourteen they will have the desire to cooperate and participate in activities with others. When they are six we teach them that throwing trash in the trash can is the right thing to do so that by the time they are sixteen they value their world enough to decide not to litter. We need to move our children from being parent-motivated to being value-motivated. Such values are not instilled overnight. To accomplish this takes an incredible investment of time and energy with long-range goals in mind.

During my daughter's freshman year in high school she had an English teacher who required her students to keep a journal. On one particular occasion, near Thanksgiving, the teacher asked them to write an entry with the title "Giving Thanks." The following essay is what Anne submitted.

GIVING THANKS JOURNAL ENTRY

by Anne Savage

Do you have a good friend? No, really, a great friend who is closer to you than your friends or even your family? A friend who is closer than a brother? If you do you are so thankful for them, right? They are there through thick and thin. I am really thankful for my best friend.

My friend and I have been best friends for fourteen and a half years! He has been there through school work, play, jobs, and even boyfriend breakups. My friend's name is Jesus. He and I have known each other for quite a while now. He knew me before I was even born. I was introduced to him the minute I was held in my mother's arms and she said, "My child, you are a blessing from the Lord!" We are really good friends. He has helped me through so much in my life. A lot of girls don't get to talk to guys about their own guy problems and breakups. However, Jesus cares and actually gives me advice on how to handle my setbacks in life. He sits down with me and talks to me. He asks me how my day is going and how life has been treating me. We don't have to write letters to each other or talk on the phone. We sit face to face and talk. He comes alive to me in so many ways. Through the flowers, snow, and reading my Bible. I have had a lot of bumps on my road in life. He has always been there to pick me up. He even died for me! No other friend I have would do that! Do you have a friend like that?

My life has drastically changed because of this relationship. My other relationships are better because of the one I have with Christ. If my friendship with God isn't right, then my other relationships and life go downhill also. This can happen especially with my relationship with my family. I hear many teenagers saying they don't have good relationships with their moms or dads. Well, my relationship is great. We talk, laugh, share good times, and I even get punished when I do something wrong. I love my relationship. However, when my relationship with Christ is on the rocks, so is my relationship with my parents.

First and foremost, is my relationship with Christ. Everything is harmonized when my relationship with Christ is good. If this connection is at the beginning and end of my day, everything else just falls into place. Isn't that a great feeling of letting everything rest on One's shoulders who can handle the load and not have to worry about it?

I found Anne's journal entry by accident. She had printed off a copy to turn in and found a misspelled word. She reprinted the entry and left the first copy by the computer as usual—Anne has an aversion to throwing things away. As I read it tears came to my eyes. She got it. She really *got* it! When it came to her faith experience, I realized that she had indeed made the transition from her parents' faith to her own personal faith. That is the kind of accomplishment I'm looking for! That is one of my goals as a professional mother!

Let me tell you that this didn't happen just by taking her to church every Sunday. It happened because of prayer. It happened because of the countless books we read about Jesus' love. We started with the little square cardboard toddler books and moved to the children's devotionals we read and talked about together. It happened because of the times we saw rainbows and discussed God's promises. It happened because of the difficult times in my life and her life and the discussions we had about God's love and His truth. It happened because we prayed together—as a toddler we prayed the simple prayers and as a teenager we prayed prayers about the realities of life, friendships, and school. It happened because of time invested in the life of this child. Ultimately it happened because of God's grace.

Investing in our children does not always guarantee they will turn into the mature, godly, respectful, and loving adults we would like them to become. God gave them minds of their own and they must ultimately make decisions for themselves. Some of the best parents do have wayward children. But if we have invested in them and shown them the way, we can live without regrets. At the very least we have shown them the way to return, when they decide to return to right living.

As we work toward the long-term goal of preparing our children for adulthood, we need to break our responsibilities into short-term goals. One of the objectives of this book is to break down our long-term goal of preparing our children for adulthood into short-term goals that we can more readily achieve. This takes us to the next step in redefining accomplishment: changing our "to do" list. By doing so, we will find that we do indeed accomplish things every day!

CHANGING YOUR "TO DO" LIST

I serve on a team of four writers that writes a weekly column for mothers at home in our local newspaper. Several years ago I had the task of writing the column to be published on the annual Take Your Daughters to Work day. I decided to address this day, which is set aside to encourage young girls in their career choices. In doing so, I described the reality of my day as a mother. Here's what I wrote:

A LESSON OF LOVE

"Mom, I was left out today. The girls in my class went to work with their moms for Take Your Daughter to Work Day. I couldn't participate, though, because you don't work." Thus began the conversation I had after school one day a year ago with my then eleven-year-old daughter. It was at that time I decided I just might participate in the event that takes place each spring. Anne would spend the day in my "office" experiencing a day in the life of a mom. Our day might involve any (or even all!) of the following:

- Get up early to get ready before anyone is awake
- Get everyone off to school
- Feed the baby
- Clean up the kitchen
- Begin the laundry
- Plan meals to keep within a one-income, tight budget
- Read a story
- Pick up toys
- Fix mid-morning snack
- Clean up the kitchen
- More laundry
- Run the vacuum (the cereal is crunching under my feet!)
- Referee a disagreement
- Feed the baby again
- Bandage a skinned knee (Mom's kisses have healing power, you know!)
- Answer a "Why is the sky blue?" question

- Make lunch
- Clean up the kitchen again
- Play "Don't Break the Ice"
- Pay some bills
- Play "Don't Break the Ice" again
- Pick up toys again
- Fold laundry
- Run a kid to the dentist
- Take a meal to a new mom or a sick friend while we're out
- Bake bread for the freezer
- Clean up the kitchen (yes, again)
- Pick up toys
- Feed the baby once again
- Read another story
- Clean a bathroom (I just can't stand it anymore!)
- Encourage a friend on the phone
- Prepare an after-school snack
- Pick up kids from school
- Listen to the tales of the day
- Clean up the kitchen once more (that now makes four times today and we're not yet to dinner!)
- Begin preparing dinner
- Help with homework
- Watch the neighbor's kids for an hour
- Feed the baby (yes, again!)
- Finish dinner
- Dad's home

I'm sure the women who came up with the idea for Take Your Daughter to Work Day didn't exactly have this particular type of experience in mind, but I have a feeling Anne won't suffer in any way. In fact, she's well aware of the wide array of career opportunities that are available to her and often speaks of her lifetime goals. But is she also aware of the incredible opportunity women have to shape the life of a child? It is an opportunity that presents itself just once in a lifetime.

Oh, I forgot one thing we would probably do. I need to dig out my teaching certificate and send it in to be renewed. I might let her help me get it ready for the mail. Then I'll tell her an important story. It's a story about tough decisions, sacrifices, and allowing God to change a mother's heart. I think she'll be glad she spent the day in Mom's "office."

If indeed we are to find some new perspective about the responsibilities of motherhood, we need to evaluate what we do and the value of those activities. Our "to do" lists become less task oriented and more relationship oriented. The lists become a reflection of an investment of time spent with other people. Before I had children my "to do" list looked something like this:

- Make phone calls in morning
- Finish Project A
- Lunch with coworker
- Attend afternoon meeting
- Run to store after work
- Finish wallpapering bathroom

As a professional mom, my "to do" list looks something like this:

- Read to Austin
- Help Erica with homework
- Take Anne to library
- Take Evan to piano lessons
- Teach Austin how to match shapes
- Do four loads of laundry
- Prepare breakfast
- Clean up kitchen
- Prepare lunch
- Clean up kitchen
- Prepare dinner
- Clean up kitchen

Now I rarely make a "to do" list that looks like that, but at one time I did. I was struggling so much with feeling as though I wasn't accomplishing anything that I decided to do a "did today" list at the end of the

PROFESSIONALIZING MOTHERHOOD

day. After I completed the list, I drew a line through each activity indicating that it was accomplished. It may sound silly to you, but it worked for me. If you are a list person at all, I would highly recommend this exercise to help you change your perspective. After I did this for a few days, I switched to making a "to do" list at the beginning of the day that included the things I valued doing as I invested in my children and my husband. Here's how my two lists compared:

REVISED "TO DO" LIST

(Reflecting Goals I Have as a Professional Mom)

- Read to Austin to further expand his world
- Help Erica with homework to assist with her education
- Take Anne to library to aid her in completing her school project
- Take Evan to piano lessons to further develop his talents
- Teach Austin how to match shapes to help grow his mind
- Do four loads of laundry to take care of the physical needs of my family
- Prepare breakfast to give my family a good start to the day
- Clean up kitchen to take care of the home I've been given
- Prepare lunch to provide for the nutritional needs of my family
- Clean up kitchen to model the value of taking care of what we've been given
- Prepare dinner to give our family a time to sit and talk and be refreshed

I think you get the picture. We need to rethink what we do and why we do it. Jean Fleming addresses this in her book, *A Mother's Heart*, when she says,

> The aspect of mothering that excites me most is knowing I am making a permanent difference in my children's lives. I am a woman of influence. I impart values, stimulate creativity, develop compassion, modify weaknesses, and nurture strengths. I can open life up to another individual. And I can open an individual up to life.

• 36 •

She goes on with this thought as she shares further,

> When I read my child a story I am doing far more than entertaining him. I am expanding his world with language, words, thoughts, and imagination. When I sit beside a child's bed at night to talk and pray, I'm doing far more than cultivating a bedtime ritual. I'm tuning in to what he is thinking, catching up on his day, listening for fears, hopes, and questions.[3]

Our "to do" lists are not something I believe can be done simply with quality time. I believe it also takes a quantity of time. We can't underestimate the value of being there for our children as they journey to adulthood.

Quality time for four-year-old Austin is doing a puzzle with him. Quality time for ten-year-old Erica is watching her on the trampoline. Quality time for fourteen-year-old Evan is listening to him play his piano music, while quality time for sixteen-year-old Anne is sorting through the challenges of teenage relationships in the evening after dinner. All of these activities have great value. If I were to measure them by the world's standards of accomplishment, though, they wouldn't measure up. If I measure them against my long-term goal of investing in the lives of my children and ushering them through childhood into adolescence on their way to adulthood, then I am right on target. I have used my time and talents wisely.

HEARTFELT APPRECIATION

One afternoon a man came home from work to find total mayhem in his house. His three children were outside, still in their pajamas, playing in the mud. Empty food boxes were strewn all around the front yard. The door of his wife's car was open, as was the front door to the house.

Proceeding into the entryway, he found an even bigger mess. A lamp had been knocked over and the throw rug was wadded against one wall. In the front room the TV was loudly blaring a cartoon channel and the family room was covered with toys and various items of clothing.

In the kitchen, dishes filled the sink, breakfast food was spilled on the counter, dog food was on the floor, a broken glass lay under the table, and a small pile of sand was spread by the back door.

He quickly headed up the stairs, stepping over toys and more piles of clothes, looking for his wife. He was worried she might be ill, or that something serious had happened. He found her lounging in the bedroom, still curled up in the bed in her pajamas, reading a novel. She looked up at him, smiled, and asked how his day went.

He looked at her bewildered and asked, "What happened here today?" She again smiled and answered, "You know every day when you come home from work and ask me what in the world did I do today?" "Yes," was his incredulous reply.

She answered, "Well, today I didn't do it."

I love that story! It illustrates the unique responsibilities of one who cares for the needs of children. It also illustrates the lack of appreciation for the tasks unless, of course, they are left undone. Thus, we find the last challenge of feeling a sense of accomplishment—feeling appreciated.

Our society equates advancement in the workplace with work done successfully. A financial bonus, an incentive, or, at the very least, a regular paycheck gives an individual the feedback that his or her efforts have been successful and appreciated. These rewards are present in most jobs outside the home. In the profession of motherhood, however, they are absent.

On a daily basis we find simple appreciation, though, in the little things: snuggling on the couch, a bouquet of dandelions, and pictures for the refrigerator door. Success is found when a toddler learns his colors or shapes or a teenager navigates a tumultuous year of high school with the help of after-school talks with Mom. These are the rewards for our efforts. If we don't watch out, we'll miss them! These accomplishments won't be rewarded with a pay raise, a certificate, or a new office. Instead you'll find reward in a smile, a hug, or a gentle squeeze of the hand.

We are valuable. The years committed to the profession of motherhood do have benefits. The benefits just look a little different than the benefits paid employees might receive. Most important, the key to finding appreciation in our profession is to understand our worth. We must understand our value in the world and we must understand our value to the God who created us.

The profession of motherhood is very much a serving profession. A decision to take care of our families' physical and emotional needs dictates our primary responsibilities. In the midst of taking care of others, though, we can't neglect ourselves. Let's continue to shift our thinking as we identify and address our own physical and emotional needs as women in the profession of motherhood.

——————— A STEP FURTHER . . . ———————

Define your long-term goals as a professional mother.

◌◌

List some significant accomplishments you would like to achieve that would show you are making progress toward your goals (e.g., expressions of thankfulness or compassion, confidence, specific skills learned, etc.).

◌◌

Create your own "to do" list of tasks that need to be done, then expand it to show the value those tasks have toward achieving your goals.

chapter 3

Take Care of the Caregiver

Any occupation whose primary responsibilities include caring for the needs of others is usually accompanied by wonderful relational benefits. These same occupations can be very emotionally and physically draining and require a plan for refueling. As we all know, motherhood has twenty-four-hour-a-day, seven-day-a-week responsibilities. While there are no designated days off, vacation time doesn't seem to be addressed in the job contract either. If we don't take some time for ourselves, if we don't arrange for a day off here or there, or if we don't take an evening for ourselves, we will find ourselves in a hole that is difficult to climb out of. We may lose our perspective or even consider reentering the paid workforce just to keep our sanity. As a woman in the profession of motherhood, you must learn how to take care of yourself. No one has built that into your job description and no one is going to set boundaries for you. You have to do it yourself.

As moms, too often we work sacrificially and selflessly to the detriment of our family life. It's then that we become short-tempered, judgmental, and even jealous of those who have more freedom in their lifestyles. We find ourselves discouraged with the daily duties of a job that never feels finished. We begin to question the value of what we're doing and our self-worth. To combat such reactive emotions, we need to be proactive in caring for ourselves.

Have you ever been on an airplane and listened to the instructions about using the oxygen masks in an emergency? The flight attendants always give special instructions to those traveling with children: Put your own oxygen mask in place before you place the mask on your child. Those directions seem to go against our very nature. Our first inclination is to take care of that child even if it means sacrificing ourselves. But when we stop to consider the reasoning behind the instruction, it makes sense. If we don't take care of ourselves first, we might not be able to help either one of us and we might both perish in those few precious moments. If we put our mask in place first, we are then in a position to care for others.

The same principle applies at home. We must first take care of ourselves in order to properly take care of others. This will give us the stamina, patience, and perspective needed to care for the needs of others over the long haul.

PULL INTO THE FILLING STATION

Do you have someone in your family who insists on driving the car on gas fumes when the gauge is registering empty? It seems every family has one member who pushes it to the limit. Well, each one of us has an emotional fuel tank. If we don't take time to fill our tank, if we push ourselves to the limit, sooner or later we will find ourselves "out of gas." Stranded. Stuck. Ineffective.

We're broken down along the road and someone has to come take care of us. By that time, it takes more to fill us up. If we're proactive, we do something to fill up while we can still pull up to the gas pump.

Moms are always taking care of others, but we have to make sure that in the whirlwind of life we're taking care of ourselves as well. There are three personal areas we need to care for: body, mind, and spirit. Do you know how each of these is drained and filled? To keep our lives balanced, we need to evaluate these areas regularly and place emphasis on keeping our tanks filled as we do the job God has called us to do.

TAKE CARE OF YOUR BODY

When Anne, our oldest, was born, I was twenty years old. Mark was twenty-four. We were both young and full of energy. I could study into the night, be up with the baby, and still go strong the next day. When Austin, our youngest, was born, I was thirty-two. My body didn't have quite the same stamina it had had three babies earlier. I needed to pay attention to its limits or my body would require me to take notice.

How much sleep do you need? Are you getting it? The body regenerates itself through the process of sleep. When we short-circuit that rest time, it breaks down the body's natural self-care cycle. Do you need to go to bed earlier? Do you need to lie down in the afternoon for just a few minutes? Take a few minutes for some much needed shut-eye if you need to. You'll feel better and will be better equipped to meet the needs of your family.

What about your eating habits? Are you trying to survive on whatever your kids don't finish? Are you eating healthy food or are you in a snack habit? Our bodies need specific minerals and vitamins. A diet of peanut butter sandwich crusts does not provide the nutrients our bodies need. I'm a person who has always struggled with the three-meals-a-day thing. I'm not particularly fond of breakfast food. So if I'm going to skip a meal, it's usually breakfast. When I realized I didn't have to eat breakfast food, though, I found myself able to get a good start in the morning by eating something else. Instead of a bowl of cereal, I might have a bowl of chicken and rice soup. And no, brownies and cookies for breakfast don't make the grade. I know, I know, I've tried to make them work, too, but they just don't have the same effect. We must feed our bodies the nutrients God designed them to run on.

How much water are you drinking every day? Several years ago, I increased my water intake. I was amazed at the increase in energy and the decrease in appetite I experienced! I've never been particularly fond of water myself, so I had to be creative about making it attractive. I did this by keeping lemons and limes sliced in my refrigerator and dropping a wedge or two in my glass of water. This little splurge on myself has resulted in a physical benefit.

What about your health? I am amazed at how many women I talk to who have not had a pap smear and breast examination in years. Take these preventive measures to care for your body. It is truly a gift to your family. A very good friend of mine just finished three months of chemotherapy after a mastectomy. She's thirty-eight, married, with two young children. Thank goodness she was taking care of herself and her body. The cancer was caught early and her chances for a long life are very good.

A common habit that mothers at home fall into is not taking time to fix themselves up each day. When I first started staying home, there were actually days my husband returned home in the evening only to find me looking the same way he had left me in the morning—no makeup, hair disheveled, and dressed in sweats. It wasn't a pretty sight.

I have to admit on the days I don't take care of my appearance, I don't feel good about myself and I struggle with low motivation. We tend to fall into that pattern, especially when we're not going anywhere outside the home. I would actually ask myself, "Am I going anywhere today?" When the answer was no, my thought process was, "Why bother?" I learned over time, though, that it's important for me, my husband, and my family that I make the effort to look and feel my best every day.

Consider putting on a pair of jeans, a belt, and a blouse or sweater rather than a pair of sweats. Take a few minutes to curl or style your hair. Add a bit of makeup and some earrings. It will make you feel better. Just before your husband comes home, take a peek at yourself in the mirror and fix your hair or makeup. You'll feel good about yourself. He's worth it, and so are you.

PERSONAL CARE PRIORITY LIST

- Sleep (enough to keep you in a positive mood)
- Nutrition (food that gives you energy and keeps you healthy; plenty of water)
- Annual Pap Smear, Breast Exam, and Physical
- Hygiene—Neat hair, some makeup
- Clothing that is comfortable but makes you feel presentable (Remember, you're not going out to an office, but you are doing a respectable and very important job, so dress accordingly.)

TAKE CARE OF YOUR MIND

Dr. Brenda Hunter, author of *Home by Choice* and many other wonderful books, received her doctorate at age forty-nine. She says that it is proof that your mind does *not* rot during your years at home with your children!

At times, though, it's easy to feel that our minds are in a low gear when all we're dealing with is diapers, dishes, laundry, and Dr. Seuss books. Just as it is important to take care of our bodies, it is equally as important to take care of our minds.

I love to read the newspaper, but I have little time to do it. Therefore, my goal is to read the paper several days during the week. It keeps me informed about local and national news, and it helps me to stay in touch with the outside world. It fills my mental fuel tank.

What do you love to do that will keep your mind filled up? Read? Make a craft? Do cross-stitch? Surf the net? Talk with friends? Writing in a journal is great therapy for the mind. Find out what works for you and then carve out some time to make it happen. You may have to ask for help in accomplishing it. Be prepared for that. There was a season that I literally could not find time to read the newspaper without the assistance of my husband. From the time I got up in the early morning it was all babies and toddlers until I went to bed too exhausted to read anything other than the inside of my eyelids. The kids couldn't seem to get on the same nap schedule and I was completely depleted when Mark would arrive home. We finally talked about it, and I asked Mark if he could give me thirty minutes after he came home for me to regroup. I'd take the newspaper to the bedroom, close the door, and begin filling up my fuel tank. There were some days I would actually emerge a different person than the one who had entered the room thirty minutes earlier!

Maybe you don't have a husband who's willing to help. In that case you may need to swap baby-sitting with a friend. If you have family close by, ask Grandma or a sister or sister-in-law to help. You might want to hire a sitter to help you accomplish your goal. Remember, your mental health is important to your family's health.

There's one more area we have to consider as we care for our minds. We have to learn to limit our activities outside the home in order to keep our minds from being bogged down with things that really aren't important. Because we are at home it is often assumed that we have more free time to do volunteer work than others have. We are often asked to serve more at church, school, and so on. As we consider our commitments outside the home, it is important that we understand four concepts: good and best, learning to say no, the urgent and the important, and asking for help. If we can grasp these concepts, we can maintain a healthy balance in the responsibilities we carry.

GOOD AND BEST

You are a talented, capable, and responsible person. Talented, capable, responsible people are asked to do more. You will be in high demand to do lots of good things. But the question to ask is, "What good things do I need to say 'no' to, and what are the best things I can say 'yes' to?" You're not choosing between good and bad; you're choosing between good and best. That's a hard choice.

One way we can determine what is good and what is best is by knowing what our mission is in this season of our lives. Most organizations and businesses have a mission statement that helps them stay focused on their goals. It also allows them to know what business ventures to pursue and what needs to be left for another organization or business to develop. They compare a new idea or venture opportunity to their mission statement. They ask the question, "Does this fit with the mission of our organization?" Then they move forward from there.

Have you ever considered writing a mission statement for yourself? What is your mission in life? A good way to begin to answer that question is to ask yourself, "When I leave this earth, what legacy do I want to leave? Where do I want to have made a difference?" Now go through and list your priorities. Then take your mission statement and your priorities and begin making some goals: lifetime goals, annual goals, monthly goals, and daily goals will enable you to fulfill your mission. Your mission, priorities, and goals should be related. Now you have a grid to help you make decisions about your "best" activities.

When asked to do something, make prayer the first step toward making a decision. If God hasn't given you a strong sense of direction in prayer, the next step is to compare it to your mission, priorities, and goals. If it doesn't fit in with those, then the decision is practically made for you. If it fits in with your goals and mission, though, you will need to further evaluate your time availability.

Another way to approach decisions about activities outside the home is by asking, "What is God asking me to do in this season of my life and does this activity fit with that plan?" When I know I could do a job but I'm trying to determine if I should, I often pose this thought, "I am capable, but am I called?" Is God calling me to do it?

We don't want to overload our minds to the point of losing our focus. We also don't want to carry so many responsibilities that we shirk what God is calling us to do in caring for our families. Having a plan for making those good vs. best decisions is the first step in setting limits on activities outside the home and ultimately in taking care of ourselves.

LEARNING TO SAY NO

"So how do you do it?" she asked.

"Do what?" I replied.

"How do you say no?" she questioned.

"I just say no," I answered.

"No, I don't mean like that. Do you say no and offer an excuse, or do you just say no? I feel so guilty when I say no."

Thus began a recent conversation with a mom who called and asked how to keep a good balance between volunteer activities and family responsibilities. As mothers at home, it is not work and family we need to keep in balance. After all, our family is our work! For many of us the issue is balancing volunteer positions (church, community, and school) with our family responsibilities. Some of us figure a home-based business or part-time job into our schedule, too. We can easily put ourselves back in the position of working full-time, outside-the-home hours without bringing home the pay. We must learn to use the word *no* effectively.

To keep a balance between mothering and helping others outside your home, here are some guidelines for learning to say no.

1. *Keep in mind that you alone know what is best for you and your family*. With many mothers working outside the home,

there are fewer school, church, and community volunteers available during the day. Therefore, you are likely to be asked more often, simply because you are perceived to be more available. Remember, even with church activities, that our families are our first ministry.

2. *Never say yes on the spot.* Always tell the person you will call back after you've had time to pray and think about it. This keeps you from making an on-the-spot decision you may regret. You can say no immediately, however, if you know that the position or responsibility is wrong for you.

3. *When considering a time commitment, make sure you take preparation time into account.* Most of us underestimate the time it takes to really do a job. If you have been asked to bake five dozen cookies, look at the calendar and determine whether you truly have that much free time available before the cookies need to be delivered. If it looks too busy, say you're sorry, but you can't do it.

4. *When considering long-term commitments, make sure you consider all your household responsibilities and the time constraints that accompany them.* It may seem that becoming the president of an organization you really believe in will not take too much time. But after a few months, the phone calls, meetings, and errands begin to take up the time you previously used for laundry, housecleaning, or paying the bills. These are big jobs that need to be integrated into your weekly and daily responsibilities. Don't allow your family responsibilities to be sacrificed for your volunteer responsibilities.

5. *Carefully consider the "brain space" this responsibility will require.* Have you ever been listening to your children, but really thinking about a new project or the hundreds of things you needed to do? When your mind is cluttered, you are not mentally available to your family.

6. *Remember every minute of your day does not have to be scheduled!* If you have a "doer" mentality, you will think of a spare hour or two as a way to fit in one more "yes." Yet we

need some time to do nothing. If you need to, schedule in "down time" each day. Write it on your calendar and say no to anything that would fill this time.

7. *Set a limit to the number of long-term commitments you will carry.* For instance, within the Hearts at Home organization we encourage women to carry no more than one large and one small long-term volunteer commitment. If they were to take on another long-term commitment, we would encourage them to give up one of their previous commitments. Limiting your long-term commitments allows for more time to help out in short-term service projects. You will be more likely to have the time to bake brownies for your child's classroom or be a teacher's assistant during Vacation Bible School if you take a similar approach.

8. *Ask for accountability.* Ask your husband, a close friend, or your Bible study group to hold you accountable for the number of commitments you will carry. Be open to their insight. If you have trouble saying no, ask them to help you during the first few months while you get things back in balance. When you tell someone you will call him back, check with your accountability partner first before answering. Sort through your schedule with them. Eventually you won't need the partner's help, but it can help you while you are learning to say no.

9. *When you do say no, don't feel that you need to give a long list of excuses.* You know what is best for your family and for yourself. If you feel you must give an excuse, simply say that it would not fit into your schedule at this time.

10. *Keep in mind that you do not have to say yes simply because you are capable.* You may have strong leadership skills and will most likely be asked to lead anything you get involved in. That doesn't mean you have to say yes to those responsibilities. You should say yes only after considering your time availability, other volunteer responsibilities, your family commitments, and what you might need to give up to properly do this job. Of

course, above all, you should say yes only after praying and
seeking God's will.

11. *If you have too much on your plate now, reevaluate your priorities.* Determine what responsibilities you need to let go of.
Give a one-month notice to those organizations that you will
no longer be able to serve. Although it may be difficult to give
up a responsibility, you are not doing the organization or your
family any good when you cannot fully commit to the job. As
soon as you let go of some of the responsibilities you are carrying, instill new boundaries for your time. Don't let yourself
become overcommitted again.

12. *Remember that saying no allows others the opportunity to
say yes.* Don't take service opportunities away from others.

Don't forget to make time to have a friend over, take your kids to
the park, write a letter, or go on a date with your husband. We don't
usually schedule these kinds of activities, but they are the first to go
when we are overcommitted.

Remember that saying yes to some activities outside the home
will be important to your sanity. Moms of young children need to get
out of the house to socialize and think about something other than
diapers, bottles, and coupons. Contrary to popular belief, your brain
will not turn to mush. It will just feel like it at times. We need to carefully choose those activities we will be involved in so that our time
will be used wisely. You will be amazed at the patience you will have
with your family when you find balance in your activity schedule.

THE URGENT AND THE IMPORTANT

Another important concept we need to understand is the difference between the urgent and the important. The important things sit
and wait while the urgent things scream to us. The phone is a perfect
example of this. A conversation on the couch with your husband is
important. The phone call in the middle of it seems urgent. Our
nature is to choose what seems urgent because we react immediately
rather than thinking about the choice we have and determining the
best thing to do.

es and goals can help us to determine what is impor-
out life the urgent will scream louder than the
use Arndt writes about this in her book, *A Mother's Time*.
says:

> The urgent matters of life are those that demand our immediate response, the things that constantly bid for our attention. They give no consideration to what is presently being done. They include annoying interruptions at the wrong time for the wrong reason and the pressing needs of people around us. These are the urgent matters of life.
>
> While the urgent continually begs for our attention, the important keeps silent. It patiently waits for us to take notice. While the urgent seeks us, the important waits to be sought by us. The important aspects of life take discipline to perform, while the urgent are accomplished on impulse.
>
> We live in constant tension between the two, don't we? Filling the needs of the moment causes us to become weary. We blame hard work for our anxiety. In reality, it is not hard work that produces stress, but doubts and misgivings about what we are doing. We have become slaves to the urgent.[4]

Are you with me here? Can you see how the urgent takes us away from the important? So what do we do about it? Discipline is the key. We started with the phone at our house. My husband and I discovered it was robbing us of the important. It rang while we were reading to a child, it rang during dinner, it rang when we had company, and we always answered it. We decided that the phone was the urgent and the things it distracted us from were the important. So, if you call my house, you often get my voice mail. If you are visiting, you will hear the phone ring a lot, but I won't answer it. Believe me, you'll stop hearing it after a while. It just begins to blend in with the background. With one husband and four children, there is a lot of "important" to take care of. The "urgent" can be called back at a time when I am needed less by those who are important.

When you start thinking about what you need to do and categorizing it as urgent or important, it can help in decision making, too. We need to discern rather than react.

ASKING FOR HELP

I can't do it all. You can't do it all, either. We must learn to *ask* for help. Our families are not mind readers. They will not know what needs to be done around the house. But you know. So, we must ask for help and delegate some of the work.

In our home, our children have family responsibilities they take care of each day. Some people might call them chores, but I don't believe that truly describes them. It takes a lot of work to keep a home running. We have a responsibility to teach our children life skills they can take with them when they leave home. So, each day they have responsibilities that help keep our home running smoothly. Those responsibilities include cooking, cleaning, laundry, yard work, and so on.

There is a lot to do, but when many hands work together, it makes my load lighter. A good manager delegates tasks, and as a professional a mother must do the same. I also have to train my "workers," and that takes time. But it is time well spent because our family benefits from the results for years to come. We need to become comfortable asking for help.

Several years ago, Mark and I decided we needed to get serious about having some date nights for ourselves, but we didn't have the money to pay a sitter on a weekly basis. We decided to *ask* some friends to commit to trading nights out. It worked out wonderfully and we enjoyed the exchange for several years.

It took me a few years to figure this out, but I'll share it with you just in case you haven't yet discovered it. Your husband can't read your mind. I thought for sure my husband could for years. In fact, I'd often help him along with some body language and a few nonverbal hints but he just wouldn't get it. I learned I had to state clearly what I needed and ask for help when necessary.

Elisa Morgan, author of *What Every Mom Needs*, puts it this way, "We have to learn to help ourselves. We have to learn to ask—directly, by using words. No one can read your mind. No one is going to waltz in, recognize your predicament, and save you."

YOU KNOW YOURSELF BEST

I learned several years ago that I respond to specific external factors when it comes to stress management. For instance, I love muted lighting. It causes me to feel warm and relaxed. Even more than that, I love candles—especially sugar cookie scented candles. Their glow and aroma seem to reduce my stress. I also love quiet. I don't want the radio playing or the TV running for no reason.

What do you like? What calms you? What kind of atmosphere is beneficial to you? Know those things about yourself and make them happen as often as possible. These are small but effective ways to take care of yourself.

I once did a call-in radio show called *Midday Connection* with Andrea Fabrey. As we talked about the profession of motherhood, a young mother called in. She shared that she was very tired and felt both emotionally and physically depleted. She said the baby slept several times during the day, but she felt she needed to work hard during those nap times. She stated this would "earn her keep" for staying home. She felt guilty taking a nap. I asked her if she needed permission to take a nap. Did she need someone to tell her that was a perfectly acceptable way of taking care of herself so she could take care of her family? She said she had never thought about that. I told her, "I give you permission to take a nap. Do it for yourself, do it for your husband, do it for your baby." We need to know ourselves, our needs, and our limitations. Then we need to adjust our lives to take care of ourselves.

Maybe you're doing a great job of taking care of yourself. If so, wonderful! But my interaction with women tells me that we don't routinely do a good job of taking care of ourselves. In fact, most of the time we wait until we've crashed, either emotionally or physically. Or we wait until we blow our tops. Or we just plain old wait until our tanks are empty and we have nothing left to give to our husbands and children.

As you begin taking care of yourself, you'll be amazed at the change in energy, attitude, and effectiveness you'll experience. Most important, your job satisfaction will soar to new levels.

The career of motherhood is very demanding. The work is worth it, but it necessitates knowing ourselves, setting boundaries, and taking care of our minds and our bodies. As we grow in our career of motherhood, we must respect the unique needs of this particular profession. We must excel at caring for ourselves. To do this effectively, we need to learn about the Person who wants to take care of us.

OUR SOURCE OF STRENGTH

All the things we've talked about are very important, but if we neglect the One who truly can meet our needs, we will always be looking for more. We must understand our value in Christ. Taking care of a family involves mundane chores. It is repetitive work. And it is exhausting. But God's Word is designed to fill us up. He wants to give us rest. He wants us to pull up to His pump and to fill our tanks by being in relationship with Him. He wants to encourage us with His Word.

When it comes to taking care of yourself, God says, "Here, I want to take care of you. Will you let me? Will you grow to know me more? Will you let me share life with you? Will you let me into your world?" Understanding our worth in Christ is the most important part of taking care of ourselves. He is the Ultimate Filling Station. He will help us keep balance in our lives. He loves us unconditionally.

───────── **A STEP FURTHER . . .** ─────────

Take this quiz to help you evaluate how well you are taking care of yourself. Use this scale to determine your answers:

5 (all of the time); 4 (often); 3 (some of the time); 2 (not very often); 1 (never)

____ I get a physical, including a breast exam and pap smear, every year.

____ I eat a well-balanced diet and drink plenty of water.

____ I know what activities fuel me and I participate in them regularly.

_____ I know how to say no, and I'm careful about my commitments outside the home.

_____ I ask my husband and children for help.

If your score is

20–25—Good job! You really know how to take care of yourself!

15–19—You have some good habits in place, but keep working to better care for your needs.

10–14—It's time to take your physical and emotional needs seriously. Make some changes today, before it's too late.

5–9— You are on the way to burnout. Go back and reread this chapter, and make new goals to reflect care for your physical and emotional needs. It's possible that you're not enjoying the profession of motherhood very much. As you make positive changes to care for yourself, you will find that your job satisfaction will increase over time.

෨

Write a mission statement for yourself. Use these questions to help you determine your statement:

• When I leave this earth, what legacy do I want to leave?
• Where do I want to have made a difference?

෨

List the people and activities in your life in order of most important to least important.

• Does your current time and energy expenditure reflect your priority list?

Identify three ways you can make adjustments in how you spend your time to better reflect your priorities.

1.
2.
3.

ᑲᓄ

Are there any volunteer activities you need to let someone else do to bring more balance to your life? List those here and begin the resignation process this week.

1.
2.
3.
4.

ᑲᓄ

Identify two of the twelve points in the "Learning to Say No" section that you want to remember in the future. Share them with a friend and ask her to hold you accountable.

part 2

DETERMINE YOUR STRATEGY

chapter 4

DO YOU KNOW YOUR TRUE VALUE?

How much of what we do as mothers is valued by the world? Reading book after book to a toddler, changing an infant's diaper ten times throughout the day, and doing twelve loads of laundry a week can often chip away at our self-worth. If we redefine accomplishment and garner a new perspective on the value of motherhood, we are making an important shift in thinking for this career choice. As we set our strategy for success, there is an important area we need to explore. The true value of a mother at home is not only found in what we *do*, but in something much more important. We need to understand the true value of who we *are*.

WHAT IS A MOTHER WORTH?

When you consider all the jobs a mother takes on and the cost to hire someone else to do them, her net worth far exceeds an annual income of $100,000. A mother is a laundress, housekeeper, nurse, interior decorator, chauffeur, purchasing agent, cook, and counselor, just to mention a few jobs that would command a high salary. Additionally, she provides services that you can't put a price tag on: rocking the baby, kissing the hurt, hugging each child, answering endless questions, praying for the family, educating little ones in God's Word, giving spiritual training, just to name a few.

The profession of motherhood is more than a variety of tasks; it involves a higher calling. It is a calling to invest years in the life of another. It is a calling to love unconditionally. It is a calling of sacrifice. Being at home is truly a job that is often taken for granted by others. A sense of accomplishment can often escape us. It's hard labor with no monetary pay. It's certainly not highly valued by most of our society.

The profession of motherhood actually calls for us to go against the tide of "me-ism." It requires a serving heart and a willingness to give. *If we are to keep our vision throughout the years of motherhood we need to have an understanding of our worth beyond the tasks and sacrifices we make.*

Our true value is found in a personal relationship with Jesus Christ. It truly does not matter what I do—it matters to whom I belong. It does not matter what I sacrifice—it matters what He sacrificed for me.

Being at home with children can be a job filled with mundane chores. Days become months in which we may feel little sense of accomplishment. Appreciation is scarce at times. Our value cannot be determined by what we accomplish, but rather by what can be accomplished through us. It is through a relationship with Jesus Christ that we can truly become the mothers we want to be and the mothers God wants us to be.

GOD HAS A PLAN FOR US

My kids have a children's music tape they have listened to over and over again. It's by "The Donut Man," Rob Evans, who sings simple children's songs about God's love. His theme song is one of our favorites: "Life without Jesus is like a donut, there's a hole in the middle of your heart!" are the words that he sings throughout the song. It's such a simple thought, but the analogy is so true!

God designed us. He designed life. He is the author of relationships. He has a plan for us to have a personal relationship, a real friendship, with Him. When we try to live life without Him there is a hole in the middle of our hearts. There is a void in our lives. There is a space we keep trying to fill with everything except God.

Some of us try to fill that space with possessions. Some of us attempt to fill it with position. Others try to feel fulfilled with money. Still others hope to fill the void with superficial relationships that contribute nothing to their personal or spiritual growth. Many of us use food, alcohol, or even drugs to fill the emptiness in our hearts.

Have you ever sat with a toddler learning how to put shapes in a bucket? The goal is to match each shape with its corresponding hole. First we put the triangle in the triangular hole. Then we move on to a rectangle, a circle, and a square. If we try to put the triangle in the circular hole it won't fit. It's not designed to fill that space. That's the way our lives work, too. There is a God-shaped void in our hearts that is designed to be filled with a friendship with Him. When we decide to live in relationship with God we find it is just what we've been looking for! It's the piece that provides the fulfillment we have desired. We are whole when the hole is filled with God.

People can't provide that fulfillment. They will always disappoint us. Possessions can't fill the void because we never have enough things. God is the only one who can fill the space in our hearts and satisfy our longings. And as we grow in relationship with Him, we can become the mothers we want to be.

GOD'S UNIQUE DESIGN

God has created us to live life in relationship with Him. We are not merely puppets, though, with God pulling the strings. He has created us to make life and eternity decisions on our own with His guidelines setting the direction. God sent His Son, Jesus, to die for us. He loves us so much that He gave His only Son, that whoever believes in Him will not die, but have eternal life. That is a powerful love! It's a perfect design.

The choice is ours. Our answer to whether we believe in Him or not will impact life now and our eternity as well. When we follow God's guidelines, we are able to enjoy His intended peace and fulfillment.

When we choose to go our own direction, we are left to experience the consequences of our often selfish decisions. Life with Jesus is just what we are looking for, even if we didn't know we were looking for it!

Linda Weber describes this well in her book, *Mom, You're Incredible!*

> When we speak of being a good parent, of being a nurturer and encourager, there's no better model than God Himself. Who loves like God? Who has sacrificed more than God? Who has provided for our future more than God?
>
> He has given us life. He is the sustainer of life—He provides every breath we take. He is the one who longs for our friendship with Him. He's the one who will always sit with us through our pain, our sorrow, our fear. He's our comforter. He's the one who nudges us toward good things and warns us, through our conscience, away from evil things.
>
> He's the one who is always forgiving, always loving, always waiting. He enjoys our growth and aches with us over our pains. He is *for* us.[5]

I can't think of a better friend than that! This is the friendship we each desire. We are designed to live life with God. Linda goes on to say,

> Think for a moment about the perfect mother. What characteristics would describe her? Maybe humble, wise, content, generous, self-sacrificing, peaceful, gentle, loving. But wait a minute. How can that be? How can she be content and peaceful if she has been sacrificing, giving, and loving? What about her fulfillment? What about her rights?
>
> . . .That's why we need God. The world around us tells us we have to look out for number one, demand our rights, and stand up for ourselves. Then we'll be happy. The result has been people who are more and more self-centered and selfish and yet, at the same time, less satisfied and still unhappy.
>
> God tells us to go just the opposite direction of what seems so logical. He says to think more of others than ourselves, to give ourselves away, and to be generous, forgiving,

and loving. He says that in being concerned for others, we'll find ourselves satisfied whereas in being concerned only for ourselves, we'll never be satisfied.

That's not logical to a world demanding its rights. But it makes all the sense in the world (literally) to someone who stops and really thinks it through from God's perspective.[6]

God's ways are different from the world's ways. We need to understand that if we are to realize our true value both as mothers and as people. He loves us differently from the way people will love us. It is in His love that we will find our fulfillment.

WHERE DO I BEGIN?

I was raised going to church every Sunday. Through my childhood I learned a lot about God. Now I realize the huge difference between knowing *about* God and *knowing* God.

When I was twenty-one years old and a new mother, my friend Jamie introduced me to reading the Bible and to the insight it would give me as a mother. I knew *about* the Bible, but I didn't *know* the Bible. I didn't understand that it was applicable to me as a wife and a mother. I desired wisdom and I wanted help. I began to understand that I couldn't be the wife and the mom I wanted to be until I learned to live with God as my best friend. So I began a journey that I'm still on today: a journey to know God.

Think of it in a friendship sense. Maybe there's a new neighbor you've seen out with her children on occasion. Maybe you've even said hello. You've conversed with another neighbor about her and found out where she moved from, how many children she has, and what she does with some of her time. But thus far, you only know about her. You don't know her.

One day she calls and invites you over for lunch. You talk, ask questions of one another, discuss thoughts and feelings, and for the first time you are moving past the point of knowing about her to knowing her. Your relationship grows as you spend more and more time together.

It's the same way with God. We can know about Him or we can know Him. When we begin to know Him in a personal way, He promises us a life that is not lived alone. He also promises us eternal life in heaven. If you have never told God you want a friendship with Him, do it now. All it takes is honest words from your heart such as, *"Lord, I've tried to live life on my own and I don't want to do that anymore. I admit that I need you. I accept your friendship. I want to know you, God, not just know about you. I want to find my self-worth in knowing that I belong to you. I want to accept the free gift of salvation you offer through your Son, Jesus Christ. Thank you, God."*

We first have to accept God's invitation for friendship. In the book of John in the Bible, chapter 3 verse 16 says, "For God so loved the world that he gave his one and only Son, that whoever believes in him shall not perish but have eternal life." If we accept His invitation, then we begin our journey to know Him.

I AM LOVED AND ACCEPTED

My friend Cathy is a single mother who considers motherhood her profession. She runs a daycare service in her home to provide for the financial needs of raising her daughter. The challenges of being a single mother are not the only hurdles Cathy has faced. Cathy lost her parents at an early age and she grew up in the foster care system. At that time there was the belief that a child should never bond with the family with which she lived. Therefore, Cathy changed foster homes several times during each year of her childhood.

Growing up, Cathy didn't understand the "anti-bonding" philosophy of the foster system. What she did understand was that she would live somewhere for a few months only to be moved to a new home just as she was settling in at her current location. The system called Cathy a model child, a "good kid." In her young mind, however, she began to link the moves with behavior. She thought she was being moved each time because of something she was doing wrong. She began to head down the road of perfectionism, hoping that maybe, if she were good enough, she could just stay in one place for a long time.

Cathy and I are in a moms' small group together and we've been reading and discussing the book *The Power of a Praying Parent* by Stormie Omartian. Recently we were sharing our thoughts on the chapter about praying for our children to feel love and acceptance. Cathy was struck with the realization that all those years in foster care eroded any feelings of love and acceptance she might have had. Now that she is an adult and knows God, she has been learning how God is different from the foster care system. His love and acceptance are not based upon our behavior, but rather on grace. His love is unconditional love. She continues to battle the old thought pattern that she needs to earn love and acceptance, but daily she is growing to understand God's character more fully.

God wants us to know that we are loved and accepted. What would it take for you to understand your value to Him, and how would that make you more effective in your profession of motherhood? Many of us do not feel worthy of that kind of love. If you were raised in a home that was filled with condemnation, you may find yourself feeling as Cathy did. If you were consistently reminded of your weaknesses by a parent or stepparent, you may struggle to understand unconditional love and acceptance. If you were told you could never do anything right, you may find yourself in a mindset that says you are unworthy of God's love.

God wants us to mother with love and acceptance. He wants us to love our children unconditionally. He desires for us to model our parenting practices after Him. For us to do that effectively, we need to understand acceptance and experience love ourselves.

I AM FORGIVEN

Most of us who are in the season of mothering children grew up in a time when right and wrong started to become blurred. I remember as a teenager clearly hearing society's messages about right and wrong being personal decisions. Absolute truth became relative truth. If you felt something was right for you, then it was right. There was no right or wrong unless you decided it was right or wrong.

As adults many of us live with the consequences of our bad decisions: sexual promiscuity, children before marriage, abortion, or sexually transmitted diseases. Many of us experimented with drugs or alcohol in an effort to feel accepted by our peers. Some of us continue to struggle with addictions or related health problems.

At the time we made these bad decisions, consequences were not a part of the picture. Now we live daily with those consequences or, at the very least, with less-than-ideal memories. We may even continue to beat ourselves up over these decisions we made years ago.

God has given us right and wrong for a reason. We find our direction for life in His Word, the Bible. But He has also given us a way to bring closure to the mistakes we make in life. He designed the process of forgiveness for us to find relief from our failures.

When we begin a friendship with God, we tell God we are sorry for our mistakes (sins) and we are forgiven. We can leave the past behind and look to the future. If we were to bring up a past mistake to God after we have asked for His forgiveness, He would say, "I don't know what you are talking about," because His forgiveness is complete. He wipes the slate clean. If I live in friendship with God, I am forgiven.

Forgiveness is part of a healthy family. Just as we are forgiven, we are to extend forgiveness to those around us. God models forgiveness for us and we are to follow His lead.

I AM CARED FOR

Mark and I didn't have a dishwasher until our sixth year of marriage. By the time we moved to a home that had a dishwasher, we had two small children. I so enjoyed the respite from the task of washing dishes three or more times a day. When we added child number three to our family, for the first time I could put bottles in the dishwasher rather than trying to clean them out with a bottle brush in a sink of soapy water. It was wonderful—a simple pleasure, but a pleasure nonetheless.

Fast forward two years. As with all appliances, our dishwasher eventually saw its last day. Mark and I evaluated our finances and determined there was simply no money in the budget for a new one. We were still trying to get out from under debt we incurred early in our marriage; therefore, we were committed to paying cash if we were to get a new dishwasher. No matter how we tried to make it work, it simply wasn't going to happen for this one-income family.

I pouted for a few weeks, lamenting over the inconvenience. I wanted that little appliance—it made my life so much easier! I tried to figure out any way we could make it happen—including taking on additional debt. Each time Mark and I discussed it, we agreed that we just needed to go without it for the time being.

Over time I found there were some benefits of going without this appliance of convenience. We spent more time as a family after each meal, washing and drying the dishes together. We told stories and we laughed. We connected as we completed this mundane chore.

We had survived almost nine months without a dishwasher when I mentioned it to a new friend. She laughed as I told her about my initial frustrations. I shared with her the new joys we had found but also how I missed the convenience. She asked me if I had prayed about it. "Pray for a dishwasher?" I responded. The thought hadn't crossed my mind. God had more important things to handle than dishwashers! She suggested that I pray for a dishwasher. If God had one in mind, He would lead the way. If not, we would know that the sink and soapy water were His plan for now!

I honestly had not asked God for something so trivial before. It seemed silly, but I decided to give it a try. I wanted to strengthen my friendship with God. This was going to be a new level in our friendship. I began praying about the possibility of God providing a dishwasher for us.

Several weeks passed. It was a Sunday morning. Mark and I had driven to church separately that morning because he had to arrive early for his children's ministry responsibilities. As I drove home, I found myself at an intersection where I would normally make a left-hand turn to go home. In a split second I made the unlikely decision to go straight and make a left-hand turn at the next intersection. It was still a direct route home; it was just one I never took.

As I drove down the street I noticed a man rolling a large appliance out to the road on a dolly. I thought it looked like a dishwasher, but I couldn't imagine that it really was. (Oh me, of little faith!) I pulled into a driveway and turned around for a second look. As I approached the man's driveway I could see that this was indeed a dishwasher and there was a sign on it: "Dishwasher—$50. Works great." I couldn't believe it. I approached the man, who was now working in his garage, and asked him if there was anything wrong with the dishwasher. He said it worked fine, but they were redecorating their kitchen and it didn't go with their new color scheme. His wife wanted a new one.

At this point in our lives, $50 was still a challenge, but we could come up with it. Mark had recently done some odd jobs for a friend who had paid him for his time. It would cover the cost of our new dishwasher exactly. I told the man I would take the dishwasher and promised to return within fifteen minutes. I finished the one-mile drive to our home and arrived just as Mark was pulling in the driveway. I was so excited to tell him what I had found. I was even more excited to share with him my experience of praying for the dishwasher and having God lead the way!

That dishwasher became a tangible reminder in our home of just how much God cares for us. He doesn't care just about our needs, He even cares about our wants! The experience moved us to a new level of friendship with God. Now I share this story very cautiously because God is not some big vending machine where we deposit a prayer, push the right button, and get our prize. He doesn't work that way. But He does care about us and He does have a plan for us. We need to talk to Him about our lives, our relationships, our needs, and, yes, even our wants. As we share our hearts with Him He will reveal His plan for our lives.

God cares about the things you care about. No matter is too trivial to bring to Him in prayer. The Bible says that God cares about everything in our lives. He knows us intimately. He even knows how many hairs are on your head! He cares about your child who refuses to potty train. He cares about your husband's job. He wants you to talk to Him about your wayward teenager.

As you determine your strategy for the profession of motherhood consider this: We can't be perfect mothers, but we can partner with a perfect God. It's a winning strategy for sure!

─────────── A STEP FURTHER . . . ───────────

What baggage are you carrying from mistakes in your past? Take some time to talk to God, ask for His forgiveness, and accept His love.

૭૭

What would it take for you to realize your value to God? How would that make you more effective in your profession of motherhood?

૭૭

How have you short-changed God in His desire to care about the little things (like dishwashers!) in your life? What do you need to talk to Him about? Take a few minutes to discuss those things with Him right now.

chapter 5

IS YOUR FAMILY MARRIAGE-CENTERED?

IT WAS VALENTINE'S DAY, 1994. MARK BEGAN HIS DAY WITH THE MEN'S group he led every Tuesday. This Tuesday was different, though. After the group dismissed for the morning, one of the men pulled Mark aside. He explained that he had won a sales promotion and he had earned three trips for two to Rome, Italy. He and his wife would use one set of tickets, an employee and his wife would use the second set, and he wondered, would Mark and I like to use the last set of tickets for this all-expenses-paid trip? It was an opportunity only God could provide!

Mark immediately said yes (of course!) and then proceeded throughout his day thinking through all the details of taking such a trip. Our children were nine, six, and three at the time. Childcare was an immediate concern, so he called my parents, who live three hours away, to see if they would be available to stay with the kids for the eight-day trip. (Yes, he was working all of this out before he ever told me about it!) They said they would be happy to come. He checked his of vacation time availability and put in for the days off. Then he began to create a Valentine's card for me, which cleverly let me know of the opportunity that was being extended to us.

He thought he was "Mr. Valentine, 1994"! What husband wouldn't want to come home and tell his wife they were going to Rome, Italy, all expenses paid, no less! It was certainly something this one-income family had never even dreamed of! But this poor fellow couldn't have been prepared for what he was to encounter when he arrived home.

He was beaming as he entered the house. I knew he was up to something! He told me to sit down and explained that he had something to give to me. He pulled out the homemade card and asked me to read it. Inside it said:

> Happy Valentine's Day! We have been given a trip to Rome, Italy. It's an eight-day, all-expenses-paid trip that will take place the first week of April.
> Isn't God good? I love you!
>
> *Mark*

I couldn't believe it! I thought he was joking. But he went on to explain how his buddy had made the offer that morning, how he'd already taken care of childcare and requested the vacation time, and how excited he was to have such a trip offered to us!

I was speechless at first. But when I finally found my voice, my first words were, "I can't go."

My head was spinning with questions: How can I leave the kids? What about Erica? She's just three years old—she needs me! How can we possibly be on the opposite side of the world from our children? (My fear of flying kicked in at that point, too.) I'm not spending thirteen hours in an airplane! And I'm certainly not flying over the ocean! I can't go.

Oh, was I in for an incredible lesson! God wanted me to grow through this opportunity. He wanted me to understand something about the roles and responsibilities to which He had called me. God called me to be a wife first. Then He gave me the role of mother. His design for the family is for it to be marriage-centered. But I had not understood that design, and as a mother I had become child-centered. I had placed the children before my husband. God was going to use this trip to get me back on track with His plan.

When we buy a new product for our home, it usually comes with an instruction book, written by those who created the product. As the designers they created it with a specific purpose in mind, they fully understand how it is supposed to work, and they precisely know the limitations of using the product. So it is with God and the instruction book He left us: His Word, the Bible. In living life God's way, we have the benefit of following the directions of the One who created us, marriage, and children. He knows how it all works best. The Bible tells us everything we need to know about living life the way the Creator designed it to work.

The book of Genesis sets the priorities. First, God designed each of us as individuals. Then He gave us to one another in marriage. Finally, He allowed for children to enter the family. The marriage is designed to last a lifetime while the child-rearing season of a family's life lasts just twenty to thirty years. The marriage is the cornerstone relationship of the family—not the children. Unfortunately, though, many of us have this turned around.

I did go on that trip to Italy. We spent five days in Rome, one day in Florence, and two days traveling. Most important, we spent eight days just as husband and wife. It was just the two of us. I was reminded of the value of this foundational relationship for our family. And I learned the importance of being a wife first and a mother second. The trip was the catalyst I needed to get things back in order.

We were created to have God as our first love. God then designed the marriage relationship as the cornerstone of the family. Finally, children both enter and leave the family unit.

In a world filled with a myriad of messages, it is easy to get priorities mixed up. We often place our activities or the busyness of life before time with God. We place things before people. And many of us place our children before our husbands.

As you consider your strategy for the profession of motherhood, you must stop and consider where marriage fits into the picture. Often a wife gets into the trap of thinking, "My husband is an adult and he can take care of himself." On the other hand, "My children urgently need me, and they are my primary responsibility." What you need to remember is this: *Your children need you to build a strong marriage, which is the cornerstone of the family. When your marriage is stable, their world is stable. A strong marriage is a gift you must strive to give your children.*

John Rosemond, a columnist, put it well, "Some women, when they become mothers, act as if they took a marriage vow that said 'I take you to be my husband, until children do us part.' Today's wife sees her husband as a parenting partner, there to assist her in what she perceives to be her primary responsibility."

We must invest time in our marriages. When we give time to something, we're saying "This is important." Nobody is going to give us that time. We have to carve it out ourselves. We have to look at the calendar, call up the sitter, make the arrangements, and follow through on our plans, no matter how much work it takes to get there. It is worth it! As much as we'd like to, we can't wait for our husbands to make the first move. We have to do it, because it is important and vital to building a healthy relationship, which in turn provides stability for our children. We have to do it because it builds intimacy in our relationship. Marriages are just like cars. They have gas tanks. If we don't take the time to fill up our tanks, we will eventually run out of gas and find ourselves broken down on the side of the road.

After years of placing my children first and my marriage second it became a habit that was difficult to break. But it was possible to change. When children first enter our families, our attention does change. Some change is out of necessity. Life is different when a child enters the scene. That doesn't mean we should put the marriage on autopilot. It doesn't work that way. Relationships of any kind don't work on autopilot. The husband-wife relationship must be grown purposefully. A plan of action must be in place to keep it on the front burner. It has to be prioritized or it will deteriorate amidst the busyness of life.

For the marriage relationship to last a lifetime, we must invest in that relationship while the children are still at home. If not, someday we will wake up in an empty house next to our husband and say, "Who are you?"

This is contrary to the way our society operates. We are a very child-centered society. Often children enter the home and suddenly life revolves around them and marriages are put on the back burner. We also live in a society with a staggering divorce rate. Could our errant child-centered philosophy be contributing to that? I believe so. Elise Arndt addresses placing your marriage first in her book *A Mother's Time*.

"This may take a step of faith, especially if you don't feel you love your husband anymore or if you feel as though you are unappreciated and taken advantage of. Ask God to give you a heart of compassion and love for your husband, a heart that looks beyond his faults to see the strengths that attracted you to him in the first place. Aren't they still there? When you choose to place your husband before your children, blessings will follow."[7]

Reminisce with me for a moment. Think about when you met your husband. What drew you to him? What caused you to want to spend more time with him? Think about the time you dated. What did you enjoy the most? Who were you in that season of life? Who are you now? Have you lost that spontaneity or happy-go-lucky spirit? Picture your husband right now. What are his strengths? Have you told him lately? Have you made him just one more thing on your "to do" list, or have you truly kept the marriage relationship a top priority? Do your children know how much you love their daddy or do they just hear about his shortcomings? Do they see you take the time needed to build a healthy, strong husband-wife relationship? Commit today to work toward that goal!

BECOMING THE WOMAN GOD WANTS ME TO BE

Mark and I teach several marriage workshops each year. When we introduce ourselves, we often say, "We've been married seventeen years, seven of them happily." I wish that wasn't the truth, but it is. We had a rough start in our marriage relationship, and the first ten years were extremely difficult.

Anne came along when we had been married barely twenty months. My child-centeredness kicked in immediately. But that was only part of the problem.

Neither one of us came into marriage with good conflict resolution skills. Mark struggled with passivity and rage. He had also been exposed to much pornography during his younger years. I had a very judgmental heart. We had both been sexually active before we were married. Forgiveness was foreign to us. About year seven of our tumultuous marriage, we crashed. We were both tired. Love had left our relationship years earlier—we didn't even like each other. We were at a crossroads and we had to make a decision. Were we going to leave things the same and operate as roommates? Were we going to divorce? Or were we going to seek help for this damaged relationship?

We both believed that God had designed marriage and divorce wasn't in His plan. We also felt if God said it was doable, then it must be. But we had a lot to learn.

When Mark and I teach our marriage workshops we talk about the need to have "new internships" in a marriage. You see, the home we grew up in serves as our internship for life. It is where we learn about marriage, conflict resolution, expressing emotion, and so much more. When we marry and begin new families it is helpful to stop and consider the internship we experienced growing up. What did you learn in your internship that was good? What do you want to pass on to your children? In what areas of life do you need to do a new internship?

This was where Mark and I had to begin. We chose to seek help for our hurting relationship. We began to understand the areas where we each needed to do new internships. Slowly we began the process of putting the pieces of our marriage back together.

A CLOSE LOOK AT MYSELF

Mark had brought much baggage into our marriage relationship. I brought my own set of problems into our marriage, but I didn't have as many new internships to do as Mark did. This brought much opportunity for finger-pointing into our relationship, and I became an expert finger-pointer.

I wasted several years letting Mark carry the load for the mess we were in. *After all, he was the one who brought so much baggage into this marriage,* I thought. But I was doing just as much damage to our relationship with excessive judgment, unforgiveness, and unresolved anger. These were the areas of my life where I needed to do a new internship.

I clearly remember the day our marriage turned around. It was the first day I took ownership of the damage *I* was doing to our relationship. I was reading my Bible and ran across a passage I had read many times before. On this particular day, though, the words of Matthew 7:3–5 jumped off the page at me. Here's how I read it:

> Why do you look at the speck of sawdust in your husband's eye and pay no attention to the plank in your own eye? How can you say to your husband, 'Let me take the speck out of your eye,' when all the time there is a plank in your own eye? You hypocrite, first take the plank out of your own eye, and then you will see clearly to remove the speck from your husband's eye.

God had a message loud and clear for me. He took the plank that was in my eye and hit me across the head with it. It was time for me to shut up and shape up. That day my prayers changed from "Lord, change him," to "Lord, change me."

This was the turning point in our marriage struggles. Do you know why? Because for the first time I left Mark alone and he ceased having to defend himself. After he stopped walking on eggshells waiting for me to come down on him, he began to feel freed up to work on the changes God was asking him to make. The very changes I was asking him to make, I actually kept him from making, because he had to spend so much energy defending himself to me that he had no energy left to spend on positive change.

A NEW INTERNSHIP FOR ME

I had much to learn. Most of us do. The question is whether we're willing to invest in whatever it takes to make changes in our thinking and our behavior. I began the process by reading whatever I could about being the wife God called me to be. God's Word is filled with many instructions concerning marriage. Additionally, I found many good books to assist me in the process. And then, finally, I set myself up in accountability relationships—women whom I asked to hold me accountable for my attitudes and actions. I also began making more effort in our counseling appointments.

I wish I could tell you it was all smooth sailing from that point on. I must report, though, it was exactly the opposite. It got worse before it got better. Stick with me here, please. You see, for the first time we were actually working through our issues instead of just bringing them up, arguing the same old arguments, and tossing them aside unresolved. It was the resolution of our issues that took so much time and energy. Thankfully, we were committed to working through each issue until we found resolution no matter how long it took.

Sometimes resolution was found in apologies and extending forgiveness to one another. We also worked hard to determine new ways we would handle situations in the future and we grappled with communicating our differing thought processes and agreeing on compromises. It seemed as though we were moving at a snail's pace at times. There were moments it felt as though we were even moving backward instead of forward. But we were making progress, and we were committed to continue working through the issues with the help God was giving us.

HAPPILY EVER AFTER?

Although it felt as though Mark and I would never get through all of our big issues, we eventually did. Most important, though, we learned how to work through conflict on our own. We began to listen to one another. In admitting our faults, we began to ask for and extend forgiveness.

Do we still have our share of problems today? We sure do. The difference is that now we know how to work through them and we have the tools needed to do the job. And oh, how good it feels!

Do you need to do some woodworking? You know, got any planks to remove from your eye? Have you been too busy trying to remove the splinters out of your husband's eye? I challenge you to back off if that has been your habit. Your role is not to operate as the Holy Spirit in his life. God can do that job just fine without you. Your responsibility is to be the woman and wife God is calling you to be.

Has your marriage been put on the back burner? Are you operating in your marriage as if your marriage vows said, "I take you to be my husband until children do us part"? Do you need to place your husband at the top of the "to do" list? Now is the time to do that. Not tomorrow, but today. Begin preparing yourself to meet him when he comes home. Call a sitter and set up those date nights you've been intending to have. Arrange for the kids to go to Grandma's or a friend's for an overnight and kidnap your husband for a surprise getaway.

It is time for us to be wives first and mothers second. If we don't do it when the children are home, we may very well not have a marriage when the children are gone. Furthermore, when our children know that Mommy and Daddy love one another their world is stable. They find security in knowing that Mommy and Daddy take time for one another and care about one another. Finally, the example we set for our children will be what they take into their marriages. We are the overseers of their home internship. We must show them a healthy balance and relationship.

If your relationship needs improvement and you are the only one who sees the need for changes, please don't become discouraged. Focus on who God wants *you* to become. Pray for your husband and respond to him in a godly way. At the very least you will feel good about yourself and the progress you are making, not to mention what might happen when you get off his back. You may find, as I did, that the energy your husband spends defending himself against your accusations, judgments, or anger is just the energy he needs to work on some of the changes he needs to make.

God has a wonderful plan for marriage. He designed the relationship Himself and gives us the "how to" to grow a strong, healthy relationship. Let's get our priorities in place and make marriage the cornerstone of our families. It is a strategy that always wins!

──────── **A STEP FURTHER . . .** ────────

Is your family child-centered or marriage-centered? List three goals or actions that will assist you in making your marriage a priority. (For example, weekly or biweekly dates, being willing to leave the children for a while, putting the children to bed earlier.)

୧୨

While you were growing up, what did you learn in your home internship that was good? What do you want to pass on to your children? In what areas of life do you need to do a new internship?

୧୨

What plans do you have for investing time in your marriage this month? How about an overnight getaway this year? Take the time now to make some plans for putting your marriage first!

chapter 6

WHERE ARE MY COWORKERS?

WHEN BEGINNING A NEW JOB, IT PAYS TO KNOW OTHERS IN THE INDUS-try. When my husband's career was sales, he made an effort to get to know other people in the business. When he left sales and entered the ministry, he made sure he knew the other pastors in town. When I was teaching, I knew the other music teachers in the area. Have you ever asked yourself *why* networking is so valuable? For me, this allowed for shared ideas and shared resources. It also provided encouragement. Knowing other teachers in the area kept me from feeling isolated in my duties. It was an opportunity to keep my perspective, work through my difficulties, and be challenged in my work.

The career of motherhood is no different. We need to know others who are doing the same job we're doing. We need other women to help us sort through the challenges of life. We need access to shared resources and shared ideas. And we need to know that we are not alone.

NETWORKING: A KEY TO STAYING HOME

When I first entered full-time motherhood, I would frequently tell my husband, "I'm the only one working in my office!" What I was really saying was how isolated I felt at times. I was communicating how I missed the interaction with coworkers. I missed the impact of having other adults in my life. What I didn't understand, though, was that I didn't have to give up adult interaction for good. *I simply needed to find a new network of coworkers for my new career.* The key to finding that network is learning where to look.

In order to find other women in the career of motherhood, you must begin by going places where other mothers go. You must also be determined to step outside of your comfort zone to approach women who are in the same profession as you. Before we talk about where to find your network of mothers, let's talk about the unique situation women at home are in when it comes to networking.

When I was teaching music privately, I often had a waiting list for piano and voice students. Whenever I could, I would recommend another teacher to students on my waiting list. When I heard about new teachers in the area, I would call them and introduce myself as a fellow music teacher. I found out specific information about the teachers, their schooling, what they specialized in, and their fee structure for private lessons. I also let them know about music teacher associations in the area, contests and performances in which they could involve their students, and the best music shops in town. My goals were not only to know what these fellow musicians could be bringing to the city and to me as teachers, but also to introduce them to what we had to offer.

When our goal is to meet other mothers, it seems a bit awkward to approach networking in the same way. When I called a new teacher I would say, "Hi, I'm Jill Savage, and I'm a music teacher here in town. I understand you are also teaching music, and I wanted to find out some specifics about your studio." This introduction opened the door for more discussion, more questions, and ultimately more information to be exchanged. When I meet another woman who I believe is doing the same job I'm doing, it seems rather silly to say, "Hi, I'm Jill Savage, and I'm a mom. I understand you are a mom, too." That doesn't seem to work as well. So let's talk a little bit about our approach to networking.

I once read in Dear Abby, "There are two kinds of people in this world: those who walk into a room and say, 'Here I am!' and those who walk into a room and say 'There you are!'" What a profound statement! As we will see, it is the key to understanding how to network with other moms.

When you start a new job, you are introduced to coworkers. When you begin the career of motherhood, you have to introduce yourself to coworkers. And you do that best by determining to find out about them first.

When we have a "Here I am!" attitude, we are waiting for people to come talk to us. We are waiting to be approached. And most often we will end up being disappointed. When we have a "There you are!" attitude, we move beyond the self-conscious, self-focused, and even self-centered approach to meeting people. Our goal becomes finding out about the other person. This immediately puts the other person at ease since people usually love to talk about themselves. After we've had the opportunity to listen for a while and learn about this other person, we can share a bit about ourselves. The doors of communication have been opened, and we can now begin the process of networking.

Not every woman we come in contact with will become a best friend. She will, however, be an important part of the mothering network in your area. As you meet and interact with other mothers at home, you will build a community of mothers that will become a valuable support system.

PEANUT BUTTER AND JELLY SANDWICHES

Meeting other moms is the first step, but if we don't go any further than the initial process of meeting someone, the relationship will never move from acquaintance to friendship. The next step we need to take is inviting someone to spend time with us. We need to invite another mom and her child(ren) over for peanut butter and jelly sandwiches.

Too many of us break out in a nervous rash just thinking about inviting someone to our home. We fret over the house and the food. But really the very thing we are looking for, friendship, is what most other women are looking for, too. The house and the food really don't matter, but the friendship that may develop does.

Do you desire to spend time with other moms? Do you have trouble getting it all together to invite someone over? Here are some ideas to get you started:

- Don't worry about having a perfect house. No one has a perfect house. Don't worry about picking up all the toys—they're all going to get pulled out anyway!
- If you invite someone over for lunch, forget about making a huge spread of food. The friendship is what she's looking for, not a gourmet meal. Peanut butter or grilled cheese sandwiches always taste wonderful when shared with a friend.
- Don't worry about a meal at all. Invite another mom over and bake cookies together or have a cup a tea.
- When having a guest in your home, concentrate on making her comfortable. This will take your eyes off of yourself and allow you to concentrate on her needs rather than your insecurities.
- When hosting a friend and her child in your home, don't be afraid to instruct the child or communicate to the mom about the guidelines in your home. Boundaries can be kindly communicated about keeping food in the kitchen or not jumping on the furniture.
- If having someone in your home completely stresses you out, invite another mom to enjoy a local park or the McDonald's Playland with you and your children.
- When at the park or Playland, strike up a conversation with another mom by asking her how old her kids are, how long she's lived in the area, and what she did BK (before kids!). If you seem to hit it off, exchange phone numbers and agree to get together again. Then be sure to call her!
- Consider doing just a moms' night out. Ask another mom to join you for pie at a local restaurant.
- Invite another mom to join you for a movie.
- Ask a friend to work together on a garage sale.
- Hearts at Home Conferences make for a great weekend away. Ask a friend to join you at a conference event.

Meeting other women is just the first step. Inviting someone to spend time with you is how a relationship is nurtured and able to grow. Friendships take time, energy, and a willingness to step out of our comfort zone. But, it is so worth it! Why don't you invite someone over for peanut butter sandwiches today? You'll be glad you did!

MOM2MOM

We started our moms' group with eight women. Eight who wanted to have some regular interaction with other moms; eight who desired to learn more about being wives, mothers, and homemakers. Eight who desired to be "family" for one another. We met every Wednesday morning in my living room, and we hired a college student to watch our children while we met. Eventually we called our group Mom2Mom.

We laughed together. We cried together. We learned together. The moms in my group proved to be the most important relationships I had outside of my family. My time spent with other godly women inspired me to be the wife and mother God called me to be.

Moms' groups are becoming more and more prevalent in cities around the world. MOPS (Mothers of Preschoolers) has set the pace with their groups designed specifically for mothers of preschoolers, and the concept of mothers gathering together to network with one another is growing rapidly. There is a tremendous need for such organized groups in women's lives. They provide instant camaraderie. They help connect women in the profession of motherhood, and they open the doors for friendship opportunities.

There are two different kinds of moms' groups that are equally effective. Large, structured, and often church-sponsored groups are one kind. Small, unique, and often individually organized groups are another.

LARGE MOMS' GROUPS

The value of a large group is primarily in developing a connected and networked "mothering community." When women know they can gather on a regular basis to meet with other moms, a sense of community is built. Such interaction provides networking opportunities that dissolve the isolation so many at-home mothers struggle with. It also provides camaraderie that helps moms feel encouraged about the job they are doing.

Large moms' groups are usually best supported by a local church. This allows for a place for children to be cared for and ample meeting space for the mothers. Large groups usually have anywhere from twenty to two hundred women involved. These are considered "open groups," as new women are welcome to join year-round.

If you are specifically looking to connect with mothers of preschoolers, then MOPS is the first place to start. Check out their website at www.mops.org to see if a group is available in your community. If not, you may be able to charter a MOPS group. In doing so, you will be given the materials and resources to create a successful group to meet the needs of mothers of preschoolers.

If you are looking to connect with a wider age group of women (women who have preschoolers and women who have school-age children) you may need to create a group of your own. Although Hearts at Home does not sponsor moms' groups like MOPS does, we do have resources available to assist groups in getting started.

When it comes to curriculum for large groups, volunteer guest speakers can provide good programs. The topics may range from parenting to marriage, cooking to cleaning, and prayer to understanding the Bible. Many moms' groups exist as a Christian outreach to the community. These groups provide a Christ-centered, practical environment for moms to find education, encouragement, and friendship.

Childcare is often the biggest challenge for most large moms' groups. Consider these ways to meet the childcare challenge. Rotating moms in the childcare rooms is one possibility. Hiring workers is another option (if you live in a college town, students studying early childhood education make great sitters), and a third possibility is finding an older women's group who is willing to take on the childcare as a service project.

Large groups need good, strong leadership to keep the group on task and to keep the leadership accountable to godly ways. Having set guidelines for relationship management, specifically conflict resolution, is also a key to keeping moms' groups effective.

SMALL MOMS' GROUPS

An equally effective moms' group arrangement is the small-group setting. Small groups usually have no more than six to eight women involved and are considered "closed groups." In other words, once the group is formed, no additional women are added to the group for a specific period of time. I've known some small groups that have been together more than ten years, and others that operate on a one to two-year commitment with the goal of "birthing" new groups after a year or two.

Women in small groups are brought together by a leader who organizes the group. Groups may meet weekly or once every other week to encourage one another, pray together, and challenge each other to be better mothers and wives. Relationships are built quickly in a small-group setting as women have the chance to regularly share their hearts and their lives.

Because of the small numbers in the group, the program is often based on a study or a book the group reads together and discusses. Some groups enjoy watching a video series. Childcare is not a big issue with small groups because many meet in the evenings when dads are home.

Small groups work well when the mothers involved are in the same season of mothering (preschoolers, school-age children, teenagers, etc.). The women find a sense of connection and camaraderie as they spend time together. They can also learn much from one another.

If you are looking to connect with other mothers in your community, consider the possibility of joining or forming a moms' group. Both large groups and small groups meet the needs of many women who consider motherhood their profession. There are other groups that don't fit either of these categories. Moms in Touch International (MITI) are small groups of moms who get together weekly to pray for their local schools, the children, and the teachers. Coffee Break, Community Bible Studies, and Bible Study Fellowships are all nationwide programs of community Bible studies for women within a church. These programs have childcare for infants and/or programs for preschoolers. While all of these groups have specific goals in mind (praying for schools and studying the Bible), any group you join will enable you to get to know other moms and form a network. And of course, the simplest group to form is the old-fashioned play group, in which a group of moms gets together at a house (rotating) or park each week, and while the kids play, the moms chat about their profession!

A COMMUNITY OF MOTHERS

In my early years of mothering, I took any opportunity to be with other women who were also in the profession of motherhood. I knew I needed to find a new network of coworkers. I searched for women who were both in my same season of motherhood and those who were a step ahead of me. Having much to learn, I set out to find the community of women who could assist me in my job.

Dr. Brenda Hunter addresses the importance of taking pride in the profession of motherhood in her book, *The Power of Mother Love*. In her book she talks about the importance of "a mothering community." She states,

> Years ago I heard the late British psychiatrist John Bowlby speak. That day he told the audience that all mothers of young children need to be mothered themselves, especially those who are wounded. He called this 'mothering mom,' indicating that the more support a mother has the better mother she will be.

"Mothering mom" is not a new idea. It's one our culture did naturally for years. As women married and became mothers, they were naturally mentored by their mothers and grandmothers who lived nearby. They learned not only the skills of homemaking, but also the values of teaching and training children, and how to be the wife God called them to be.

In today's transient society, though, we have lost the natural process of family mentoring. Many young wives and mothers do not live near their extended families. They find themselves isolated from their family connections. Furthermore, women who do live near extended family may find themselves alone in the motherhood profession as their mothers and grandmothers are employed outside their homes.

Our culture has raised the demand for building a community of mothers because of the nature of our lifestyles. The basic need for women to learn about homemaking, parenting, and marriage has not disappeared. It is still there, but the avenues previously available to teach these skills are often no longer available. This is why MOPS groups, moms' groups, and Hearts at Home are so important. They are about the business of mothering moms.

Women in the profession of motherhood need a strategic plan for networking. Look in the right places with the right attitude—this is the first step to find new coworkers. Next, move from acquaintances to friendships. Finally, seek out organized communities of mothers. This rounds out the essentials of your networking strategy.

After we complete a shift in thinking, a good strategy provides the foundation for success in the profession of motherhood. After the foundation is laid, we can move on to understand the tools of the trade as the next step in building a successful career in motherhood.

—————————— A STEP FURTHER . . . ——————————

Would you describe yourself as a person who walks into a room and says, "Here I am!" or a person who walks into a room and says, "There you are!"? What changes can you make to more often respond with "There you are!"?

ೲ

List three moms you would like to get to know better. Invite one over for peanut butter and jelly sandwiches or a cup of tea. Invite another to join you on an outing with the kids. Invite the third one out for pie and coffee.

ೲ

Contact Hearts at Home (309–888–MOMS) to see if there is a moms' group or MOPS group in your area. Build your mothering community by seeking individual and group relationships.

∽

If you belong to a moms' group, consider registering your moms' group with Hearts at Home. A simple phone call will help us connect other women in your community with your moms' group. Call 309–888–MOMS today!

part 3

TOOLS OF THE TRADE

chapter 7

FUN: YOU'VE GOT TO HAVE A GOOD TIME!

SEVERAL YEARS AGO, MARK PUT TOGETHER A SMALL TOOLBOX FOR ME TO keep in the house. He included the basic tools I might need in his absence: hammer, screwdriver, wrench, pliers, and a few nails and screws. He has an array of tools out in the barn that he uses as he builds and repairs things around our home. I needed the basic tools that would equip me for jobs that I came across on an average day: hanging a picture, opening the battery compartment on a toy, repairing a broken necklace.

Each profession has its own set of tools for the trade. Teachers, plumbers, accountants, secretaries—they all have tools that are essential to the job they do. Motherhood is no different. There are some basic tools we need to have for our trade. These are the tools that will make the job easier and more fulfilling. When these tools are in our toolbox and available for daily use, we will find them invaluable to the job we are doing. In this chapter and the following five chapters, we will look at six basic tools every mom needs.

LET'S HAVE SOME FUN!

My friend Cathy is one of the funnest moms I know. (Yes, I'm aware that "funnest" is not really a word. It is the made-up word used by Cathy's daughter Erin to describe her, so I think I should use it as well.) Immediately after a rain, Cathy's idea of a good time is running with the kids to the retention basin near their home and splashing in the temporary lake that has formed. I tease Cathy about being a big kid who forgot to grow up. But seriously, when did we moms forget how to play? When did we determine we were too old to have fun?

My friendship with Cathy reminds me of the need to fully enjoy this season with my family by simply having fun. Many times I take life too seriously. I'm always thinking about what needs to be done or what I need to fix for dinner, and I miss out on the times when I need to play.

Did you know that the average four-year-old laughs four hundred times a day? I have a four-year-old, and I do believe the statistic to be true. He finds humor in the simplest things. He loves to be tickled. His favorite game is one he made up himself called "Frogger, Frogger," which consists of running back and forth between two points in the yard. Oh, to find such joy in the simple things in life! We can learn so much from our children—if we will just pay attention to the lessons before us.

Playing begins when our children are small, continues when they are in grade school, and is still an important part of family life when the children enter the junior high and high school years. It seems like a concept such as having fun should come easily, but, as I speak to mothers across the United States, I find that I am not alone in this challenge. Too many of us have forgotten how to have fun. We need to have a refresher course in this basic tool of the trade needed in the profession of motherhood.

MESSY FUN

There are two kinds of mothers in this world: cleanies and messies. Your ability to have fun is going to be directly related to which category you fall in. Many times "fun" means "mess." This is the first reality we have to come to grips with if we are going to have fun. When my friend Cathy splashes in the puddles with the kids, there is certainly going to be a mess. Wet, and maybe even muddy, clothes will have to be attended to. Showers or baths may be in order. If we don't have the right perspective, this will feel like an interruption to our day. The right perspective, though, is that it is an essential part of our day. Having fun with our children is part of being a mom. And dealing with messes is sometimes a part of having fun.

I fall into the "cleanie" category. The prospect of messes far too often keeps me from having fun with my children. I have come a long way over the years, but I still have more to grow in this area. I'm way too practical at times when I need to be spontaneous. God has been working with me on this one—a project I know my kids are glad He is doing. I certainly don't want to look back, after my children are gone, and say, "I wish I had loosened up. I wish I'd had more fun." I want to do that now, while I can make the change and make a difference in my kids' lives.

SPONTANEOUS FUN

A few days before school started, my kids and I made a day trip to Chicago. It's a three-hour trip from our central Illinois home that one of my two older kids had asked to make before school started. They enjoy Navy Pier, shopping at Watertower Place, and just taking in the excitement of the big city. I asked my friend Doris to accompany me on our trip. I also knew I could use an extra set of eyes and hands taking five children (one took a friend) to downtown Chicago.

As we drove north on Interstate 55, we passed a town named O'Dell. Doris stopped mid-conversation and said, "There once was a town named O'Dell. It had a very deep well." She then went on to explain that each time her family would travel to visit extended family in Michigan, they would drive this route. On one trip several years ago that she made alone with her son, she noticed the exit sign for O'Dell and made up the rhyme. Her son, Hunter, who was a preteen at the time, picked up on the rhyme and created the next stanza. They continued with more rhyming stanzas until they were laughing and enjoying this new game they created. Hunter is now sixteen, and Doris said they still play the game every time they make the trip. Her spontaneous moment of fun provided for some much needed laughter and created a new family tradition.

Sometimes spontaneous fun happens when we maximize the moments. Cathy called the other day and invited our ten-year-old daughter to her home. Her eight-year-old daughter was having a private garage sale just for a few friends. She had cleaned out her room, priced her items, and was ready to host this special event. Cathy was surprised at her daughter's business enterprise, but decided to make the most of the occasion. She helped Erin set up the sale on their Ping-Pong table in the basement and ordered pizza for the girls who were attending this private sale. Opportunities for fun happen on a regular basis—as mothers, we choose to either maximize the moments or minimize the fun.

In the midst of writing this chapter, my two youngest were quietly playing Legos together. I soon heard whispers as they were scheming their next move. In a whirlwind of motion, they ran into the room where I was writing and asked if they could go put their swimsuits on and play Legos in the bathtub. When I asked why, they responded that they wanted to build boats and see if they would float. My initial thought was no, let's not do that. But in that same split second, I asked myself, "Why not?" Yes, it means wet swimsuits; yes, it means Legos transported to the bathroom; and, yes, it could mean a water mess, but it's a lazy Sunday afternoon, so why not? Fun for a four-year-old and a ten-year-old is different from fun for a thirty-six-year-old mother. I need to see the world from their perspective and allow them the joy of having spontaneous fun.

Have you ever blown bubbles in the house? If you haven't, why not? I remember the first time my kids asked if they could blow bubbles in the house. I said no, and then really thought about my answer. Why couldn't we? What would it hurt? We have the bubble container that doesn't spill if it's tipped over, so spills shouldn't be a concern. I soon rescinded my answer and told the kids that it would be fine. Blowing bubbles moved from being just an outdoor summer activity to being an opportunity for fun no matter what season it is.

Sometimes fun means we need to think outside the box. When I thought about bubbles, they were strictly an outside toy. When I allowed myself to think more creatively, it opened up new avenues for fun.

MARRIAGE FUN

During the dating and engagement season of our relationship with our husbands, most of us can remember having fun together. The early years of marriage allowed for that fun to continue as we only had the two of us to consider in planning activities. Maybe it was golf, camping, hanging out with friends, or attending sporting events together. It could have been bowling, watching movies, or attending concerts. Maybe it was just a simple walk in the park, watching the sun go down at your favorite spot, or sharing a sundae at your favorite ice-cream parlor. Whatever it was, it was a chance to play together.

Our marriage fun sets the pace for our family fun. It also provides a healthy "marriage internship" for our watching children. It is essential to continue having fun together as a couple.

After children, though, it takes a bit more work. We can't leave it to chance—we need to make sure it happens. One of the ways we can instill fun in our marriage is to resume the dating process. Dating is simply setting up specific times to spend together. Mark and I have found three types of dating that are important for keeping fun a part of our marriage relationship:

Daily Dates—These dates are the little expressions of communication and love that happen on a daily basis. A sexy note in his briefcase. A phone call at lunch just to check in. A gentle touch on the arm accompanied with an "I love you." These little expressions of love say, "I care, and I'm thinking of you." They bring a smile to your face. They keep an atmosphere of fun in your marriage.

Weekly or Biweekly Dates—Spending time, just the two of us, is essential in remembering and expanding our identity as a couple. This time is vital to keeping communication lines open and enjoying activities that further develop our relationship as a couple. These dates provide a perfect opportunity to plan for fun. An evening of miniature golf, a bike ride together, a picnic in the park—these all keep a sense of fun and spontaneity in the relationship.

Annual Dates—A once-a-year getaway for a married couple is incredibly helpful in keeping fun a part of the marriage relationship. An overnight at a bed and breakfast, attending a marriage seminar, or taking a vacation together helps keep a sense of adventure in your relationship. My friend Lisa and her husband have incorporated a getaway into their anniversary celebration each year. She plans the even-year celebrations, and he plans the odd-year celebrations. They enjoy the anticipation of the special time spent together each year, and each person takes turns planning the fun.

You can't discuss incorporating marriage fun without addressing the issues of childcare. This has probably been the biggest challenge our one-income family has faced over the years. The question many couples ask is, "How can we get away for a few hours or a few days when we can't afford childcare?" It is possible; it just takes some creativity.

We have handled this challenge in a variety of ways over the past fifteen years. Trading sitting with another family has been one of the best ways we have found to enjoy time together without the expense of childcare. This often allowed for longer dates or overnights we could enjoy, because we were not paying a sitter an hourly rate. Of course, in exchange for that time out, you watch the other couple's children in return. This works well when you find a couple whose parenting style and values are similar to yours. It also helps if their children are close in age to yours.

If extended family lives nearby, an evening with their grandparents or a night with their favorite aunt or uncle are childcare options. To meet the financial challenges of an overnight or extended vacation, begin putting away just $10 to $20 a month to invest in your dates or getaways. It will be a wise investment that will pay large dividends of fun in your marriage.

If hiring a sitter is within your budget, consider setting up a regular date time weekly or biweekly. Most teenagers who baby-sit enjoy the regular income and the opportunity to get to know a family well. This will assure you of regularly scheduled time together and will not allow the busyness of life to squeeze out much needed time for marriage fun.

FAMILY FUN

Family fun is an important part of building a strong family identity. When families have fun together, it builds a bond that can last a lifetime. Traditions are often developed in times of fun. Those traditions help define and individualize each family.

At the Savage household, we have a tradition of fun called "surprise rides." This started when the older children were small, and we wanted to surprise them with a spontaneous activity. It might be ice cream at our favorite ice-cream parlor, a spontaneous trip to the park, or a matinee showing of a new family movie. Whatever it is, though, the anticipation is the best part of the fun. From the time Mark and I yell, "surprise ride," and everyone rushes to get in the car, until the time that we arrive at our surprise destination, the excitement increases. As the kids have gotten older, they have often suggested surprise rides. Of course they're not really a surprise that way (unless your teenager is driving you somewhere!), but the suggestion alone says, "Let's have some fun together as a family." It has given us common ground and shared vocabulary that lends to family fun.

Holidays also provide opportunities for fun that may develop into special traditions. Several years ago I served dinner backwards on April Fools' Day (dessert first!). It was a fun evening that started a new tradition. Each April 1 has been dubbed "Backwards Day" ever since.

Families need to recreate together. We need to have unstructured times of togetherness. I'm not talking about watching TV together— I'm talking about a pick-up game of basketball, playing cards, or just sitting out on the porch talking and laughing together. Camping, fishing, biking, and hiking are great times of family recreation. As moms, we must take the initiative and make these things happen. We have to be available, and we have to value having fun together. As we spend time together in both spontaneous and planned activities, we will find our family relationships growing stronger.

BIRTHDAY FUN

When Mark and I married, we both brought different traditions and definitions of fun into our new family. One of the areas in which we saw tremendous differences, was in the way we felt birthdays should be celebrated.

Mark's family celebrated birthdays with a bakery birthday cake. He especially remembers having those little candy letters and flowers on his cakes. Oh, how he loved those candies. The family often went out to dinner when a family member had a birthday. An abundance of presents topped off this annual event.

My family celebrated birthdays with a homemade birthday cake that was decorated with love. My mom made a great effort to decorate the cake just for the birthday person. She always tied in the theme of the birthday party or the person's hobbies, interests, or activities. Our birthday celebrations were most often at home and always included grandparents, aunts, and uncles. One present from the immediate family was a part of this special celebration.

Mark and I married and had no idea of the conflict we were about to experience. When I made Mark a homemade cake, decorated with love (they didn't always look wonderful, but I spent lots of time on them), and prepared him a special meal at home, he was disappointed. When Mark arranged for dinner out at a special restaurant to celebrate my birthday and purchased a bakery cake for me (yes, it had those little candies on the top!), I tried to appreciate his efforts, but I, too, was disappointed.

When our children came along, we decided we had to leave the old traditions behind. It was time to create new Savage family birthday traditions. In addition to some birthday celebration ideas that we borrowed from friends, we created some of our own. Our new traditions spell out family fun and are anticipated by each family member when a birthday rolls around.

The night before a birthday is spent preparing for a special breakfast. After the birthday person goes to bed, the table is set with birthday plates, cups, and napkins. The family presents are placed in the center of the table. Later, we quietly slip into their room and hang balloons and streamers. When the birthday girl or boy awakes in the morning, the room reflects his or her special day. As we move downstairs to the breakfast table, the best part of the celebration takes place: cake and ice cream for breakfast! Yes, I know it flunks all the tests for a healthy breakfast, but it stands the test of time for building family fun. It is certainly a favorite activity of our family, and with six people in our family it means six times a year we get cake and ice cream for breakfast!

Our birthday celebrations have become treasured traditions for our family, special memories that Mark and I realize can only be enjoyed when the children are home. We only have a short season to fully enjoy these traditions and times of fun, for far too soon our children will be grown and creating traditions of their own.

BASIC SUPPLIES NEEDED

There are some basic tools that every family needs to have fun and stir the imagination. These are inexpensive, simple resources and ideas that stimulate play and create fun. If you don't already have these on hand, you'll find you can pull them together pretty easily.

Play-Doh

Play-Doh is easily purchased at the store, but it can also be very easily made at home. Make sure and keep a good supply of cookie cutters, plastic knives, and rolling pins for maximum fun. Here are two of our favorite recipes:

Basic Play-Doh

2 c. flour
1 c. salt
2 c. boiling water (add food coloring to water as desired)
4 tsp. cream of tarter

2 Tbsp. cooking oil
1 tsp. vanilla

Cook all the above in a saucepan, stirring until it makes a ball. Let cool. Enjoy!

Edible Play-Doh

1 c. peanut butter
½ c. powdered milk
½ c. powdered sugar

Mix ingredients together with a spoon working dry ingredients into peanut butter. Place ball of dough between two pieces of wax paper and flatten. Place in refrigerator until chilled. Wash hands before playing with dough. Kids can eat the dough as they play!

Box of Dress-up Clothes

All kids need the opportunity to pretend. Providing a box of dress-up clothes is a wonderful way to encourage them to do so. You can begin your dress-up collection with some of your old clothes. The first dress-up clothes we provided for Anne were my old prom dresses. I cut some length off one of the dresses and left the other one long. Over time, grandparents, aunts, and uncles have added to the collection. We have Mark's old boy scout uniform, animal costumes that neighbors passed on after Halloween, hats, gloves, toe socks (remember those?), jewelry, bandanas (these make great capes!), ties, shoes . . . well, you get the picture. Dress-up clothes provide hours of fun for preschoolers and grade schoolers. Even our teenagers have been thankful for the dress-up clothes when they've needed an item for the school play or a special presentation that required a costume.

Craft Supplies

Glue sticks, construction paper, scissors, yarn, Popsicle sticks, and stickers are a must-have for on-hand craft supplies. Markers, crayons, colored pencils, and paints round out the basic craft needs for an afternoon of creating. If you're really brave, glitter is a favorite, too!

Celebration Supplies

Holly Schurter, a mother of eight, shared with me one time that she has a celebration cupboard. This is where she keeps special paper plates, cups, and napkins. She also keeps balloons, streamers, and other necessary celebration supplies. These are great for an impromptu party or celebration: first day of school, an A on the Math test, or any special day you want to create.

Story Supplies

Puppets made from paper lunch sacks or old socks can be created to accompany your favorite stories. Reading a story can be a time of laughter and fun if done creatively. When reading a story, make sure to use different voices for the different characters. The kids will giggle when some of the funny voices are used.

Tent Supplies

Kids will spend hours creating a house or hideout. Old sheets and clothespins are all that is needed for this kind of fun. A folding table, a few chairs, or even the kitchen or dining room table work fine for a base structure.

Miscellaneous

Sidewalk chalk, squirt guns, bubbles, and a variety of balls are also great items for impromptu play and fun. Bubble blowing soap is very cheap, but if you'd like to make it at home, here's a great recipe:

1 c. dishwashing soap
2 c. warm water
3–4 Tbsp. glycerine (found at drugstores)
1 tsp. sugar

Gently stir together all ingredients in large container. Use bubble wands for small bubbles. Wire coat hangers can be formed into circles and used to make big bubbles.

PERMISSION AND PARTICIPATION

When children are playing, they often need two things from us: permission and participation. There are many times they play well on their own, but need our permission to "make a mess." I challenge you, as I have been challenging myself, to say yes more often than no. There are legitimate "no" times, but there are far too many times we say no when it really could be yes.

In addition to our permission, sometimes children need our participation. They desire time with us. We must remember that the most precious commodity we can give them *is* our time. The time with children at home is but a small portion of our lives. We need to maximize the time now.

Having fun is an essential part of life for both kids and adults. It is a tool that those in the profession of motherhood cannot be without. When you are in the business of raising children, this tool of the trade is very necessary to stay in the profession long term, avoid burnout, and keep a smile on your face.

———— A STEP FURTHER . . . ————

Are you a "cleanie" or a "messie"? Does your style affect your ability to have fun?

☙

What activities did you and your husband enjoy before children? What activities do the two of you enjoy now? How can you incorporate daily, weekly, and annual dates to expand the fun in your relationship?

☙

On a scale of 1 to 10, rate your ability to play (1 being lowest, 10 being highest). Are you happy with that rating? What goals will you make to move higher on the scale?

Identify the ways your family plays together now. Identify new ways you would like to increase the fun in your family.

chapter 8

PRAYER:
AN INDISPENSABLE TOOL

ONE OF THE MOST DIFFICULT RESPONSIBILITIES OF MOTHERHOOD IS THE process of letting go. We do this continually throughout each child's life. During the early years their independence begins in eating and walking. Then they go to school. Eventually, they drive independently of us. And ultimately, they make the transition to a family and home of their own.

As mothers, we have this incredible desire to be with them every step of the way. We know we need to let go, yet we want to walk with them just a little longer. We feel torn as we recognize new levels of independence. We struggle with our identity as they take steps away from us. It is a bittersweet experience at times knowing that their independence is the ultimate goal of motherhood, yet wanting time to slow down.

When Anne went to kindergarten, I experienced my first lengthy separation from her. She had been to preschool the year before and she went to Sunday school each week, but this was now a daily separation. There were now other substantial influences in her life, such as teachers and classmates. Even more unsettling for me was the ride on the school bus. On the way to school in the afternoon, the bus transported just kindergartners (for their half day). On the way home, though, the bus was filled with children in grades K–6. What influences was she going to be exposed to?

Shortly after Anne started kindergarten, Mark attended a ministry conference. In the exhibit area of the conference, he picked up some information on a ministry called Moms In Touch, International (MITI). I was not familiar with this organization, but I was intrigued by the concept of this ministry. It was very simple: Gathering mothers together to pray for their children and their school one hour each week. I called the number on the brochure and spoke with Jan, a local MITI contact person. She explained to me that forming a MITI group was very simple. The goal is to have a group cover every school in prayer. After checking her records, she explained that no group existed for my daughter's school and asked if I would be interested in starting one. I told her I was interested, but quite frankly the idea of praying for one hour was overwhelming to me. I couldn't imagine what you could possibly pray about for one hour!

Jan suggested that I work on gathering some moms together for an initial meeting. She then offered to come and teach us how to pray. I accepted her offer. Little did I know just how much this would change my life.

OUR PRAYERS MAKE A DIFFERENCE

As our children grow more and more independent, they spend less and less time with us. Although we cannot accompany them through all the ups and downs of life, God can. He can be where we cannot be. He can guide when we aren't able to guide. He can protect when we are not present. Without prayer, we may feel fear, insecurity, and doubt as our children move out from under our wings. With prayer, we can feel hope, security, and trust in our partnership with the very One who created our children.

Prayer is certainly an indispensable tool for the profession of motherhood. It is a must-have while raising our children and growing a marriage in a world that is so very confused about right and wrong. Praying for our family can be likened to sending a ship to sea with its lifeboats in place. When we do not pray, it's as if we are sending them into the storms of life without even a life preserver. Our prayers do make a difference. In *The Power of a Praying Parent* author Stormie Omartian writes,

> Our children's lives don't ever have to be left to chance. We don't have to pace the floor anxiously . . . dreading the terrible twos or torturous teens. We don't have to live in fear . . . of what dangers might be lurking behind every corner. Nor do we have to be perfect parents. We can start right now—this very minute, in fact—making a positive difference in our child's future. It's never too early and never too late. . . . The key is not trying to do it all by ourselves all at once, but rather turning to the expert parent of all time—our Father God— for help. . . . There is great power in doing that, far beyond what most people imagine.[8]

For many of us, our only experience with prayer is a few sentences before meals, a few at bedtime, and maybe prayers during a church service. For others, prayer is completely foreign—something that has never been a part of life. How do we pray? Let's take a look at just how to make prayer one of your most used tools in the toolbox.

PRAYER IS MORE THAN A SHOPPING LIST

When Jan came to our initial MITI group she explained to us the different steps of prayer: praise, confession, thanksgiving, and intercession. As we prayed as a group that evening and weekly over the following year, I learned so much about prayer. The experience in the group allowed me to expand my ability to pray for my family as I applied the principles Jan taught us to my personal prayer life. That was eleven years ago, and since that time God has truly become my best friend as I spend time with Him regularly. In recent years, I have begun using ACTS (Adoration, Confession, Thanksgiving, Supplication) as my pattern for prayer. This has helped me grow my conversations with God. Let me share with you some of the things I have learned in my prayer journey.

ACTS

A—Adoration
C—Confession
T—Thanksgiving
S—Supplication

Can you imagine what kind of friendship you would have with a person if they only spoke to you when they needed something? What happens in a relationship when gratitude and appreciation is not expressed? These scenarios describe a friendship that would not go the distance. And far too often they describe a relationship with God that is out of balance. When we have a "prayer shopping list" mentality our prayers are filled with "give me this and give me that." When crisis hits our life we cut deals with God, "I promise, God, if you will help me find my lost two-year-old in this shopping mall, I'll go back to church." This isn't the full relationship God desires, though. He wants a friendship with us. He has created us to be in relationship with Him.

When God sent his Son, Jesus, to live on this earth, He not only sent a Savior, but also sent a wonderful example for us. When we read the Bible, we see time after time that Jesus spent time with God. He would leave the hectic pace of life, all the people who needed him, and he would spend time talking with God in prayer. His life was similar to ours as mothers: People were always needing him, they were always touching him, the hours he put in were long and hard. In addition, He was a teacher, a mentor, a friend, a son, and a brother. I know I can relate to most of that.

In the book of Matthew, chapter 6, verses 9b to 13, we see a time that Jesus was teaching the disciples how to pray. Many of us know this as "the Lord's Prayer." Let's look at some of this prayer and other scriptures to see examples for the ACTS prayer pattern.

"Our Father in heaven, hallowed be your name, your kingdom come, your will be done on earth as it is in heaven." This part of the prayer is adoration, or giving God praise for who He is. The word *hallowed* means "holy." When we give God praise there are several things that happen. First, we are reminded of who God is. We see His adequacy and our inadequacy. As a mother this is important. I often feel

inadequate for the job, but when I'm reminded of God's adequacy, I'm encouraged that I can do this job if I partner with Him.

How do we adore God? There are several ways. We can sing His praises—a favorite hymn or praise chorus doesn't have to be sung just in church. We can pick out a psalm of praise and read it to God (check out Psalms 8, 19, 23, 46, 95, 100, 148). We can also focus on His attributes—who He is. Here's just a partial list of who God is:

Able	Almighty	Beautiful
Benevolent	Comforter	Compassionate
Counselor	Everlasting Life	Faithful
Father	Fortress	Forgiver
Glorious	Good	Great
Healer	Helper	Holy
Hope	Just	Kind
King	Lamb	Life
Light	Love	Lord
Marvelous	Majesty	Merciful
Mighty	Prince of Peace	Provider
Rock	Savior	Shepherd
Shield	Sovereign	Strength

When we praise God we simply say, "God, I praise you because you are _____." This reminds us of how awesome God is and how He is able to help us handle anything.

During the past year, my husband has been making a career transition. This season of transition has brought with it some financial challenges. As I look back over my prayers during this time, God, the Provider, has been very real to me. I have seen Him provide for our material and financial needs in ways I could never imagine. Whether it was prompting someone to share some groceries, providing me with a speaking opportunity, or helping us to reorganize our finances, God has provided our needs along the way. During this time He has been Kind. He has been Hope. He has been Strength. I need to praise Him for all that He is.

Continuing with the Lord's Prayer: *"Forgive us our debts, as we also have forgiven our debtors."* This is the C part of the pattern: confession. As humans, we are less than perfect. We make mistakes in our marriages, in our parenting, and in our friendships. God gave a name to those mistakes—He calls it sin. He also gave us a way to put the sin behind us—confession and forgiveness. When we are honest about our sins and confess them to God, three very important things happen:

1. Our conscience is cleansed.
2. We feel the relief of forgiveness.
3. When we are totally honest about our sins, we begin to desire change in our life.

How do we do that? We are specific and call our sins by name (judgment, lying, jealousy, selfishness, coveting, stealing, and so on).

When I was first learning about the importance of being honest with God about my sin, God gave me the opportunity to really put this into practice (of course!). I was struggling with a long-time friendship that was changing. I had enjoyed a close relationship with this friend during my early motherhood years. We traded sitting, spent many hours together, and talked on the phone quite often. Eventually, though, I began to realize that she was spending more time with another friend and less time with me. I didn't know what to do about the change. I asked her if I had offended her in any way. She said I had not. I tried to process the change, but found myself angry and bitter. As I was sorting through this one day in my mind, God spoke to me very clearly. He pointed out the mistake I had made. He showed me the sin in my heart. I was jealous.

The Bible is a manual for life through which God gives us many guidelines for the way we are to live our lives. The most well-known guidelines are the Ten Commandments. God gave us those ten guidelines plus countless others to help us to live life to the fullest. Commandment number 10 is "You shall not covet." This simply means you should not want what others have. I was coveting the relationship my friend had with her new friend. When we break one of His commandments, we are not operating at 100 percent effectiveness. I was consumed by the jealousy. It was eating at me and affecting my friendship and even my family. When I realized what was really happening in my heart, I put confession to work. I confessed that indeed I had been jealous. I asked God to forgive me. The relief of confession and forgiveness was immediate. I had dealt with my sin.

Once I had my own stuff out of the way, I was able to look at the situation with objectivity. God allowed me to see that people approach relationships differently. For me, a friendship is for a lifetime. For my friend, some friendships are for a season. Our expectations differed. The hurt I experienced was very real and it took time to move beyond that, but I couldn't have done it without identifying my sin, asking for forgiveness, and experiencing the freedom of God's faithfulness. As it says in 1 John 1:9, "If we confess our sins, he is faithful and just and will forgive us our sins and purify us from all unrighteousness."

Conversing with God allows us to bring closure to our failures in life. God doesn't want us to continue to beat ourselves up over and over when we mess up. That's why He created forgiveness. There is incredible freedom when we live in God's forgiveness. There is also incredible freedom when we can identify wrong motives or wrong actions in our lives and have the direction to do something about it.

I spent the first few years at home with my children being jealous of my husband and his freedom. I grew bitter because he could just go to the dentist's office and get his teeth cleaned. Not me. I'd have to either make arrangements for several children or sit in the dentist's chair with one child on my lap and one at my feet.

He went out to lunch five days a week. Not me. It was grilled cheese and chips, day in and day out. He had uninterrupted adult conversation forty hours a week, while I'd have to vie for it each evening.

There is nothing wrong with longing for what might be some day, or desiring things to be a bit easier or different, but when the longing crosses the line from desire to envy, it becomes sin. When we examine our hearts and ask God to forgive our sins, we grow to know God more and more. We have to say, "I'm sorry. I don't like this in me; I want to let go of it." He offers forgiveness and grace when we are honest about our shortcomings. Through our honesty in calling our sin what it is, we find freedom, forgiveness, and growth from the mistakes we make in life.

Our sinful nature expresses itself every day as we carry out our duties as moms: we're impatient with the kids, we place judgment on our spouses, we don't tell the whole truth. God, in His greatness, has given us a way to wipe the slate clean and start over. That is the gift of confession.

Now we come to the "T" of ACTS, which stands for thanksgiving. We need to be thankful for all God is and all He gives us. Most importantly, we should understand the difference between feeling grateful and expressing thanks.

Have you ever given a gift to someone who never said thank you? Maybe you've sent a gift in the mail, and it was never acknowledged. The person who received the gift was grateful for it, but until they express thanks, the giver is unaware of the appreciation for the gift. We need to say thank you to God for all His blessings: answered prayers, changed hearts, people in our lives, and the material things He gives us.

When our children express their gratitude for something we've done for them or a gift they have received, it benefits both the parent and the child. The child expresses gratitude and the parent feels appreciated. The entire process enriches the parent/child relationship. In the same way, when we express gratitude to God it strengthens our friendship with Him. The Bible mentions over and over how we are to give thanks to the Lord. In 1 Thessalonians 5:18 it says, "Give thanks in all circumstances, for this is God's will for you in Christ Jesus." Even when things don't seem to be going "our way," we are *still* to give thanks for the blessings we do have. Maybe you've had days when your kids are driving you crazy. Be thankful that you have children! Be thankful for their health! We can always think of things to be thankful for.

The Lord's Prayer ends this way: *"And lead us not into temptation, but deliver us from the evil one."* God wants us to ask Him for help in living our lives. He wants us to speak to Him about our struggles, our needs, and even our wants. He wants to answer our prayers. He wants to guide us through the ups and downs of life. This is the S part of ACTS, which stands for supplication. Supplication is a big word that simply means a humble request, a petition. Philippians 4:6 says, "Do not be anxious about anything, but in everything, by prayer and petition, with thanksgiving, present your requests to God." It is bringing our requests before Him, praying for our needs and the needs of others. As mothers, we have much to pray about.

OUR PERSONAL NEEDS

There are so many areas of our lives that we need to be praying for: friendships, spiritual growth, character and moral issues, and even our physical health and material needs. God has so much He wants to give us, but the Bible tells us to ask. Nothing is too small to pray about. God wants to be involved in the "dailies" of our lives. Remember my dishwasher experience? God cared about my desire for an everyday household appliance. I asked for this, and He answered in His way and His timing.

God always answers our prayers, though not always the way we may want Him to. When it comes to asking for things, it is important to trust God's perspective. God's perspective is different from our perspective because He is all-knowing. Have you ever watched a parade from a tall building? Many times from that angle you can see the beginning and the end of the parade as well as what is right in front of you. In contrast to this, if you have ever marched in a parade you know that because you are in the midst of the event, you can only see what is right in front of you. God's perspective and our perspective can be described in the same way. Daily we are marching in the parade of life. We can only see what is right in front of us. We don't know what is coming up far ahead of us. We don't know how the parade will finish. God does. He has a plan for each of us that only He knows. When we ask things of Him, we must keep in mind that God alone truly knows what is best for us because He sees the whole picture. Then we can trust in His answer.

OUR CHILDREN

The needs of our children change on a daily basis. They are growing, exploring, and developing every day. They are expanding their knowledge about relationships and the world around them. They are learning obedience. As they grow older, they experience both positive and negative consequences for the decisions they make. They grow in independence and their responsibilities increase. We have so much to pray about!

In her book *The Power of a Praying Parent*, Stormie Omartian identifies thirty different themes that we need to be praying for our children. Here are just a few: feeling loved and accepted; following truth and rejecting lies; resisting rebellion; instilling the desire to learn; having the motivation for proper body care; avoiding alcohol, drugs, and other addictions; enjoying freedom from fear; rejecting sexual immorality; finding the perfect mate; and growing in faith. These are just some of the many issues we need to pray about for our children.

Cheri Fuller, in her book *When Mothers Pray*, addresses how we can pray for our children based upon their developmental stages. She suggests that during infancy we pray that our children will develop trust and a strong sense of security as they bond with us. During toddlerhood, she proposes praying that they will develop a healthy sense of independence. In early childhood, pray that they develop a healthy curiosity, learn to play well with others, and explore and create without a fear of failure. And when they are school-age, we need to pray that they discover their God-given gifts and talents. This is also when we need to pray for the development of their conscience.

With the birth of each child, I have been praying for his or her future spouse and the parents of that spouse. The person my son or daughters will some day marry will bring his or her home internship experience into their marriage relationship. I need to be praying *now* for that child's home life. I need to pray for their friendship with God, their parents' marriage, and their understanding of healthy relationship skills. It's never too early to pray for our children's future marriages!

Each morning when my children head to school, I pray for their ability to discern God's way from the world's way. I ask God to help them recall the lessons of right and wrong that we have taught them and to make wise decisions when they have choices to make.

Our children need us not only to pray *for* them but *with* them—we'll explore that further in chapter 14. Praying with and for our family members is one of a mother's most important responsibilities.

OUR HUSBANDS

When we think of our children, we think immediately of their needs. When we think of our husbands, we often calculate that they are adults and can take care of themselves. If we keep that mentality, though, we will miss out on one of the biggest opportunities we have to make an impact on our husbands' lives. Don't ever underestimate the power of a praying wife.

Our husbands work in a world that is often antagonistic toward character integrity and morality. We need to pray for our husbands to make wise choices. Men are human and vulnerable. We need to pray for their fears. Men in one-income families carry the burden of provision for the family. We need to pray for their work. Men often find their self-worth in their career. We need to pray that they will find their self-worth in Christ.

In her book *The Power of a Praying Wife,* Stormie Omartian lays out a plan to help you pray for your husband. She shares simple yet effective ways to pray for his work, temptations, fears, choices, integrity, priorities, relationships, attitude, emotions, faith, and more! When I first read her book, I was encouraged and challenged at the prayer possibilities for my marriage. She does a wonderful job of exposing your mind to all the areas that a wife needs to be praying about for her husband, as well as uplifting scriptures to pray for each area. God's Word is powerful when we pray it for our loved ones!

The enemy does not want your marriage or my marriage to thrive. He will do whatever he can to break down the marriage relationship. We have to do battle on our knees for this relationship, the foundation of a strong family.

HOW CAN I MAKE THIS HAPPEN?

When I was first introduced to prayer being a part of my daily routine, I had two small children and a third on the way. My response was,

"Great, just what I need—another task for the day." Maybe you're thinking that, too. I needed to do a perspective check, though, because prayer is far more than something to be added to your "to do" list. Jean Fleming addresses this in her book *A Mother's Heart*.

> When our children were small, my times spent apart in uninterrupted prayer were brief. But I found I could stretch my total prayer time if I allowed routine tasks to trigger prayer. Even though they're older now, I still follow this practice. As I feed the children, I pray God will nourish their souls; as I bathe them I pray they will experience the spiritual cleansing Christ provides; as I dress them I pray they will be clothed in righteousness.[9]

By working within our season of motherhood, rather than fighting it, we can be creative in finding the time needed to build our friendship with God.

Let's work with the day of a mother. Your availability of a quiet time to pray will be directly related to the age of your children. Mothers of infants and preschoolers have to be the most creative in finding time to pray. It's not impossible—just challenging.

Look for the quiet moments in your day. When your child has immersed himself in pretending for a few minutes, take those minutes to talk with God about what's on your heart. When the kids have opened up a new container of Play-Doh and seem to have their interest captured, take that time to praise God for who He is. When you are sitting in the backyard watching the kids play, take the opportunity to thank God for what He has given to you. When you are folding laundry, pray for each member of the family as you fold his or her clothing. And when you put your preschooler down for a nap, take that time for some honest confession concerning the mistakes you have made. Then bask in the forgiveness God offers. There will be days when you can spend some more time with God, but don't miss the smaller, yet important, opportunities in the meantime.

As the children get a little older, it is feasible that you will be able to make a regular appointment with God. This is time for you to read

His word, the Bible. It is time to talk with God and to listen to Him. I have found it very helpful to keep a prayer notebook or journal for these times. This is where I can write prayer requests I need to remember. It is also where I can keep my list of God's attributes to help me when I'm spending time in adoration.

Most often, I choose to write out my prayers like a letter. This helps me to stay focused and keeps my mind from wandering. I also find that my prayer journal doubles as a diary. I can go back to my prayer journals over the past ten years and see how God has grown me. We often forget what was so very important to us at one time and how God helped us through it. By looking back at my prayer journals I have a document that proclaims God's faithfulness.

In my notebook, I also keep a small stack of note cards, envelopes, and postage. If God brings people to my mind during my prayer time, I will try to drop them a note to let them know I was praying for them. I also find it very handy to keep my "to do" list right in front of me. This is helpful for two reasons. First, I pray over what is on the list, asking God for wisdom in how I use my time. I also pray that my list is flexible enough that if God sends someone my way that needs some encouragement or time to talk, I will see that as an opportunity, not an interruption. Second, invariably when we sit down to be quiet for a few minutes, we think of things that need to be done. This often happens while I'm praying. With my list nearby, I simply jot down the activity I need to remember to do, and resume praying. That way I am not distracted trying to remember what needs to be done while I'm spending time with God.

THE BENEFITS OF PRAYER

When we partner with God, we can be most effective in this profession called motherhood. Spending time with God helps us to keep our focus in this incredibly busy and often chaotic job. Prayer is a tool we cannot do without. It's much more than a shopping list for the things we want out of life. It gives us hope. It opens us to God's perspective. It keeps us on track. It gives us divine companionship—there is no better friendship than that!

Knowing God is not about religion, it is about relationship. It is about a friendship with God. Friendships are developed when we talk with one another. This is why prayer is an important part of growing our friendship with God.

Having a bad day? Share it with God. Happy about something? Share it with God. Fearful of the future? Share it with God. Filled with sadness? Share it with God. Talking with God is not about some magical mixture of poetic words, it is about sharing our hearts. We talk to Him like we would talk to a friend. We share our thoughts, our fears, our dreams, our hopes, and our desires with Him. There is nothing we can hide from Him.

"Prayer provides the key to unlocking God's power in your life," explains Bill Hybels in his book *Too Busy Not to Pray*. There is a saying we use at Hearts at Home that describes the power of prayer well: *When we work, we work. When we pray, God works.* When it comes to my life as a mother, I don't want to do it alone. I want God's help, love, and guidance with my duties. I want to let Him work in my life, in my husband's life, and in my children's lives. If I'm going to let Him do His work, I have to partner with Him through prayer.

So often the challenges of life seem overwhelming. The challenges may feel like mountains that are impossible to move. But when we take our eyes off the mountain and place them on the Mountain Mover, we begin to see opportunities instead. Jesus said, "What is impossible with men is possible with God" (Luke 18:27).

When we spend time with God, it gives us confidence in this profession of motherhood. Because we are partnering with the One who created motherhood, we can operate with a sense of certainty. When we don't know the answer, we do know the One who knows the answer. There is great confidence in that!

Spending time with God increases our compassion for others and our ability to love. God's love is perfect. It is unconditional. The more time we spend with Him, the more we become like Him. Although we will never attain perfection on this earth, we can live holy lives that are pleasing to God and we can be pleasant for others to be around. As our life intersects with the lives of our family members, friends, and neighbors, they will benefit because of the God we've been spending time with!

The benefits of prayer for our family are immeasurable. No one can calculate the benefits of prayer because they are multiplied by God's incredible power and grace. We can do nothing better for ourselves and our family than to build a friendship with God. That friendship will only grow as we spend time with God in prayer. What a wonderful tool God has given to us!

——————— A STEP FURTHER . . . ———————

What was your experience with prayer in the home in which you were raised?

What experience with prayer would you like your children to have in the home you are creating for them?

What attribute of God could you give Him praise for today? Why?

Do you need to confess anything to God right now, before going any further?

What has God given you that you have never thanked Him for? After identifying those, take a few minutes to thank Him.

Identify three things you would like to begin praying about for yourself.

Identify three needs you can pray about for your husband.

೧೨

Identify three things you would like to begin praying about for each of your children.

chapter 9

CREATIVITY: LET THE CREATIVE JUICES FLOW!

It STARTED OUT AS AN ENJOYABLE SUNDAY AFTERNOON TRIP. WE HAD VISited my sister on the campus of University of Evansville in southern Indiana. As we traveled home to Bloomington, Illinois, our three small children were becoming restless—it was time for a break. Mark spotted a city park in a town we were driving through. He pulled in to allow six-year-old Anne and four-year-old Evan an opportunity to run off some energy. Erica was five months old at the time, and it was time for her to nurse. We enjoyed the sunshine and found the cool breeze refreshing.

As the kids moved from one piece of play equipment to another, Mark played with Anne and Evan while I sat on a blanket near the car and fed Erica. They were quite a distance from where I was sitting when I realized that Mark was holding Anne, who was crying. As they walked in my direction, Mark yelled for a towel or something to help stop the bleeding. I grabbed some extra burp rags I had packed for our trip and ran to help him.

Anne had climbed on a piece of equipment that had a broken spring. Neither Mark nor Anne saw it was broken until it was too late. She flipped forward and hit her head on a bolt on the broken equipment.

It was obvious that stitches were going to be necessary to both stop the bleeding and allow this gash to heal well. We had both noticed a hospital sign when we pulled into the park so we loaded the kids up and headed to the Emergency Room.

Anne was terrified. We determined that Mark would handle the two smaller children in the waiting room while I accompanied Anne into the ER. When the doctor came into the room, he talked directly with Anne asking her how this happened and working to put her at ease. He looked at the wound and agreed that stitches were indeed in order. At the mention of the word "stitches," Anne became very upset again. She said over and over again, "I don't want stitches! I don't want stitches!" I tried to calm her down and the nurse tried to reassure her, but nothing was working.

After listening to a few minutes of protest, this very wise and creative doctor replied to Anne's cries. He said, "OK, Anne, I'll give you the choice. Would you like stitches or sutures?" Anne thought for a moment and said, "Sutures." He told her it was a deal, that she was calling the shots, and he would do sutures.

That was the end of the fear. She lay completely still while they cleaned the wound and administered the sutures. Within an hour we were back on the road.

I still laugh when I think back to that day. That doctor took a completely chaotic situation and turned it into a peaceful moment with a little bit of creative communication. He understood Anne's fear and her feeling of being out of control. His creativity allowed for the situation to be changed in a moment.

Creativity is an essential tool that is used in a variety of ways within our profession of motherhood. Let's look at eight specific needs that can be met if Mom will pull the tool of creativity out of the toolbox.

CREATIVE COMMUNICATION

Just as that doctor used some ingenuity to communicate with my daughter, we as mothers sometimes need to put a creative spin on our communication. Companies spend thousands of dollars to develop just the right words to motivate their employees or their customers. Mothers need to do the same to motivate their families.

At our house we use the word *team* to describe our family. A team is a group of people who work together toward a goal. In the same way that a sports team works toward the goal of victory, families work toward goals, too. When we think of ourselves as a team, we are more likely to chip in and help one another. Whether we're working together to do yard work or pooling our efforts to clean the house or make dinner, we're doing it as a team with each team member carrying his or her responsibility.

Another term we've used is *basics*—a general term for the basic responsibilities that need to be done each morning: bed made, room picked up, clothes in drawers, teeth brushed, and hair combed. Rather than nagging about individual parts of the morning routine, the term *basics* is a nonthreatening way of describing the details of the morning routine.

Many families refer to chores as *family responsibilities*. This also brings in a team concept and more accurately describes what these duties are. Many activities need to be accomplished to keep a home in order and running smoothly: yard work, house cleaning, feeding animals, meal preparation, kitchen clean up, automobile and home maintenance. As the children grow older, it is important that they take responsibility for some of these duties. They are family responsibilities and calling them such helps to foster an atmosphere of teaching and training.

Creative communication can also be incorporated into helping children with organization. After I was introduced to the idea of "a place for everything and everything in its place," I took the concept a step further and began using the phrase "everything needs a home." Recently a friend overheard me asking four-year-old Austin to take a certain toy and put it in its home. She was intrigued by the use of that phrase. By using the term *home* and designating a place where items *live*, family members have a clearer idea of organization. Our teenagers know that the home for their school papers is in a file on the kitchen counter, the home for boots is on the shelf in the garage, and the home for phone messages is on the message log in the kitchen.

I've seen many creative mothers use the Barney song "Clean up, clean up, everybody everywhere. Clean up, clean up, everybody do your share!" to assist their preschoolers with picking up toys. Many times we can use songs to change a less-than-enjoyable activity into a fun and pleasant opportunity. My mother used to sing a little "Good Morning" song to my sisters and me to wake us up in the morning. Many times I do the same with my children. A little bit of creative communication can go a long way in setting a happy tone for the family.

At our home, Saturdays are spent working together as a team on yard work and housework. In the past I would tell the children what their responsibilities were for the day before they had the freedom to do their own activities. I often found myself reminding them several times of their assigned responsibilities and coaxing them along to accomplish them within an appropriate time frame. One particular Saturday, I was really feeling frustrated as I found myself having to keep each child on task. I was falling into nagging communication. After they left with Mark for a short stint at the shopping mall, I pondered how I might be able to better communicate each child's duties. How could I provide clear and creative communication? I opted to put the responsibilities in writing that day, rather than verbalizing them. I made each child a small checklist of his or her jobs for the morning. I also assigned them an approximate time these jobs would take. After they returned home, I handed each one his list. I asked them to accomplish their tasks, check them off their lists, and return their checklists to me completed. I couldn't believe the difference! Each child did exactly as I asked. The communication on paper was far more effective than the old way of assigning tasks. It just took a bit of time to creatively communicate.

CREATIVE FINANCES

Living on one income today is a challenge for most families. Raising children and providing for their needs is expensive. Food, clothing, medical care, activity fees, school costs—it all adds up very quickly! It takes not only a savvy mind, but also some creativity to make ends meet.

Providing for our family's nutritional needs is one of the largest responsibilities a mother carries. How can I feed my family on the money we have available for purchasing food? This has been a huge challenge for our family of six, especially with two growing teenagers. How can I be creative with the resources I have?

Many women find using coupons and rebates helps their food budget. These activities save money on brand-name products. They do take a bit of time, but the efforts are often profitable.

Our savings have been found most often in purchasing off-brand food products. Although we still have several products that we haven't been able to find an acceptable off-brand replacement for, most of the food we purchase are generic brands that taste just as good. Over time, the family's taste buds have adjusted to the transition.

Creative food preparation is also important for maximizing our resources. When you bake a chicken and enjoy the sliced meat for one meal and prepare several dishes throughout the week with the remaining meat, you are maximizing your resources. It may take a bit more time to pull the meat off the chicken bones, but the savings is worth it.

Do you use a preprinted shopping list when you go to the store? This can result in savings as you plan and shop with specific goals in mind. Sit down at a computer and create a shopping list that lists all the items you purchase regularly in the order you would find them in the store.

When eating out, there are creative ways to cut costs. Sharing meals is one option. Most restaurants serve very large portions of food that can easily be shared. If you choose to share meals, remember that the server is still serving two people. Make sure to tip the wait staff the estimated percentage of two purchased meals.

Drinks can really add up a food tab when eating out. Consider ice water as an acceptable drink option at restaurants. Adding a lemon or lime wedge offers a nice twist of flavor.

CREATIVE DECORATION

My friend Shawn invited me over to see how she had decorated her preschool son's room. I was amazed at the simple creativity she had used! We can decorate on a shoestring budget. We just need to let the creative juices flow!

Shawn wanted to decorate Nathan's room with a jungle theme. She visualized all kinds of animals painted on the walls: a lion, tiger, elephant, and monkey. Shawn found some pictures of the animals she had in mind. After turning the pictures into overhead transparencies (a service offered at any teacher supply store or print shop), she used an overhead projector to project the figures on the bedroom walls. The next step involved tracing the projected figures with a pencil. After that, the figures were painted and details added using the pictures as a template. When the room was finished the animal figures reached from floor to ceiling in the one-of-a-kind bedroom. It just took a little creativity.

My friend and former neighbor Rita also has a creative flair for decorating. She makes a hobby out of finding old and often discarded furniture and bringing new life to it. I've seen her take iron bed frames, old chairs, and discarded tables and make them into useful pieces of furniture in her home. With the wide variety of paint products and special paint effects that are available to us, this type of creativity can be accomplished by most anyone.

Creative decorating can happen when we use pieces of furniture in innovative ways. Recently we moved dressers around in our children's rooms. After Mark and I were given a dresser for our bedroom, we passed our dresser to one of the kids who really needed more room for her clothes. That child, in turn, passed her dresser on to a younger sibling. I ended up with a small extra dresser that I first thought I'd try to sell in the newspaper. At the same time, I had been trying to figure out how to reorganize our wrapping supplies: wrapping paper, gift bags, ribbon, scissors, and tape. It occurred to me that we could move the dresser into the dining room, top it with a potted plant, and place all of our gift wrap supplies in it. It has worked better than any other organizational system I could have purchased or created specifically to organize a gift wrap center.

CREATIVE TEACHING

A mother is a child's first teacher. We teach our children language skills, we assist in writing skills, and we teach them manners and appropriate behavior. We help with learning letters and numbers. As they grow older we teach them relational skills, spiritual truths, and character values. Creativity can and should play a huge role in imparting wisdom to our children.

God has created each child with unique abilities and a unique learning style. There are visual learners, those who learn best by reading or seeing a concept in action. There are auditory learners, those who learn best by hearing someone explain a concept. Finally, there are kinesthetic learners, those who learn best by touching an object or participating in an activity. It is important that we know how our children learn and then creatively teach them the concepts we want them to know and understand.

Anne, our oldest daughter, is very much a visual learner. If I want to teach her a concept, I can give her a magazine article, show her a Bible verse, or suggest a book to read. She will learn best by reading it herself. Erica, our youngest daughter, is more of a kinesthetic learner. She wants to hold things, touch them, experiment with them. She almost always has some sort of science project going on in our kitchen. If I want to teach her a concept I need to explain it to her and then maybe role-play a bit. Yes, it takes a bit more time to do that, but it is a worthwhile effort to creatively meet the learning needs of the children God gives us.

Another way that we can creatively teach our children is by looking for "teachable moments." Making creative use of our everyday experiences can lend itself to incredible learning opportunities. When Erica helps me bake cookies, it is a perfect opportunity to illustrate and discuss measurements and the math skills they require. When Anne and I shopped together to find the perfect dress for her high school homecoming dance, it allowed us to discuss the wonderful way that God has created men (and boys) to be very tuned into what they see. The instruction I gave her helped her to make a good dress choice that would not be a temptation to the young man who was escorting her to the dance.

We can teach our children spiritual truths in the same way. Author Elise Arndt calls this "devotional living." When we see a rainbow, it can prompt us to talk to our children about God's promises

(Genesis 9:13–17). When our child has been wronged and needs to offer forgiveness, we can explain how God offers us forgiveness even when we don't deserve it. By blending learning style with the teachable moments of life, we can incorporate creativity into the lessons we want our children to learn.

CREATIVE TIME MANAGEMENT

Both moms and kids need to use their time wisely. We're all given the same twenty-four hours a day, but what we can accomplish is directly affected by how we use our time. When necessary, there are ways that we can maximize the time we have.

Several years ago, I heard a speaker comment on how often we find ourselves waiting. We wait at the doctor's office, at the hair salon, for music lessons to end, to transport kids in the carpool, we wait, wait, wait. This speaker suggested the use of a "waiting bag." A waiting bag is a perfect place for that magazine you've wanted to read. It is a perfect place for that article of clothing that needs some minor mending (and the needle and thread to do it!). It is also a perfect place for note cards and envelopes to write those thank-you notes or words of encouragement you've been meaning to write.

A friend of mine shared with me that she keeps the latest issues of her favorite magazines in her car at all times. When she is waiting for the children at a lesson, sports practice, or school activity she uses the extra minutes to read. She said that she usually makes it through the magazines by the time the next monthly issues arrive, and she very rarely finds herself frustrated when the kids are running late. Now that is a creative use of time!

We also need to teach our children how to use their time creatively. We begin by planning creative ways for the children to spend their time. We need to turn off the television, Nintendo, and computer games, and instead encourage reading, coloring, creating, pretending, and playing. During the summer, we have no TV days at the Savage home. On these days, the kids wake up in the morning and actually talk with each other during breakfast. These days, honestly, I find them more cooperative and most certainly less distracted. During the school year, the TV is seldom on simply because of homework responsibilities and school activities. Children need to be encouraged to creatively use their time.

CREATIVE GIFTS

One-income families or families on a tight budget can find gift giving challenging at times. As the children get older and are invited to more birthday parties, the expense of gift giving can increase. Often extended families increase in number annually as babies are born, thus increasing birthday and Christmas gifts. How can creativity help in gift giving?

Gifts from the heart are some of the best gifts given. An inexpensively framed photo of a grandparent holding a grandchild means much more than purchasing Grandma a new piece of luggage. A special handwritten letter from a niece or nephew can mean more to an aunt or uncle than a gift certificate at their favorite store. Thinking outside the "go to the store, buy the present" mind-set is the beginning of creative gifts.

My friend Diane shared with me recently about a gift she received when she was moving to a new city. Her friends gathered together and made her a book. Each friend had a page that featured their handprint, favorite Bible verses, encouraging quotes, common phrases they used, and a personal note for Diane. She shared how special that gift was and how she continues to reflect upon it even several years later. They certainly could have pitched in and purchased her something, but a gift from the heart is one that keeps on giving over and over again.

Rita is a new mom at home. She and I are in a small group together and have enjoyed getting to know one another. At Christmas, Rita faced her first gift-giving-on-one-income challenge. She called one afternoon, and we talked about some different ideas for inexpensive gifts from the heart. I remembered our first Christmases on one income and some of the gifts we had created and given: Popsicle stick sled ornaments personalized for extended family, sweatshirts for Grandma and Grandpa decorated with the kids' handprints, and wreaths made from scrap material. As we talked I also remembered two of our favorites gifts that are not only fun, but make the house smell wonderful: cinnamon cutouts and dried apples. If you've never tried making these, try them sometime. Here are the recipes:

Cinnamon Cutouts

1 c. applesauce
1 c. cinnamon
1 tsp. nutmeg
1 tsp. all-spice
1 tsp. ground cloves

(Nutmeg, all-spice, and ground cloves can be replaced with equal amounts of cinnamon if you do not have those ingredients on hand.)

Mix applesauce and spices into a ball of dough. Sprinkle flat surface with cinnamon and roll dough to ¼" thick. Cut shapes with cookie cutters. In preparation for hanging, use a drinking straw to punch a hole in each cutout. Place on cake racks and bake 6 hours in 150 degree oven, leaving door ajar. After cutouts have cooled, thread a 6"–8" ribbon through the hole and tie.

Dried Apples

Unpeeled whole apples
2 c. lemon juice
3 Tbsp. salt
3 Tbsp. citric acid ("Fruit Fresh" brand, the most popular citric acid, can be found in most grocery stores.)

Mix together lemon juice, salt, and citric acid in small bowl. Lay whole, unpeeled apple on its side and cut into 1/4" slices. Slice from the bottom to the top. Each slice should have a star in the middle. Soak apple slices in lemon juice mixture for 3 minutes and then place on cake racks. Bake 6 hours in 150 degree oven, leaving door ajar. After apples have cooled, they should feel leathery. They can be sprayed with an acrylic spray, if desired, but it is not necessary. Apples can then be used to decorate wreaths or a ribbon can be threaded through the star in the middle for hanging.

Both Cinnamon Cutouts and Dried Apples make great Christmas ornaments, gift tag attachments, or scented room or car fresheners. They can also be used to decorate wreaths or other craft projects.

While you're in the kitchen, gifts of cookies, candies, and quick breads are also great gift ideas. People are so busy these days that they rarely take time to bake from scratch. Gifts of homemade delicacies are greatly appreciated. These can be baked and frozen ahead of time in preparation for holiday gift giving. Wrap in aluminum foil and top with a bow to create the perfect gift for neighbors, friends, and family.

Coupon books are another creative gift. A book is designed for a family member, or even a neighbor, with coupons for which the giver will perform tasks for the recipient. When a gift such as this is given, the opportunity to serve is as important to the giver as the gift is to the recipient.

Creative and inexpensive gift giving for children is possible, but a bit more challenging at times. Our one-income family has a $10 limit on birthday gifts. It can be difficult to find children's gifts on a tight budget. The local dollar store has become a favorite place for shopping for birthday presents for our family. One of our favorite gifts for girls is a basket or bucket filled with hair accessories. Teen girls enjoy baskets of fragrant skin care products. Boys or girls enjoy a gift certificate to a movie theater or favorite music store.

Creativity can also be tapped when it comes to wrapping the gift! Brown paper lunch sacks can double as gift bags. Children can decorate bags with stickers, crayons, markers, and glitter (if you're brave). Brown sacks can be used for adult gift giving, too. Paper doilies, ribbon, and rubber stamps can turn a lunch sack into a gift bag. Other wrapping paper alternates include the newspaper comics and white freezer paper that can also be decorated by children.

Creative gifts and gift wrap can assist the tight budget of any family. They also make gift giving more personal, practical, and fun!

CREATIVE DATES

Spending time alone is a necessity for keeping the marriage fires burning. Finding affordable activities to participate in as a couple can take some ingenuity especially when finances are tight. It's not impossible—a dose of creativity usually does the job!

My friend Tammy shared a memory of trying to plan for dates when there simply wasn't much money to spend on activities. She said, "George and I had so much fun trying to come up with as many activities as possible that we could do on $15 or $20. We brainstormed together and laid out our plans to use our resources and our time wisely. It was so much fun trying to make it work!"

Dates don't have to cost a lot, they just need to provide for touch and communication. Here are some creative ideas for spending time together:

- Take a walk in the park, holding hands and talking.
- Spread a blanket on the ground and enjoy the night sky together.
- Share a root beer float, complete with two straws.
- Go golfing with him.
- Ask him to go bike riding with you.
- Share a piece of pie and discuss the day's activities.
- Take a drive in the country.
- Make a trip to the ice-cream parlor.
- Revisit the location of your first date.
- Watch your wedding video.
- Have the kids spend the night with friends or family and enjoy a quiet evening at home.

Spending time together doesn't have to be expensive or difficult, and time spent together will reap incredible benefits in the long run. Using the tool of creativity to enhance your marriage relationship is a sound investment.

CREATIVE FAMILY NIGHTS

We live in a very individual-driven culture. If we don't purposefully participate in activities that keep family members in relationship with one another, we will find that over time our family will operate more like a group of roommates than a family unit.

When Mark and I began evaluating our parenting role several years ago, we determined that we wanted to parent on purpose. We wanted to have a plan for raising our children. We wanted to make sure certain ingredients were present in our family's habits. Our desire was to look forward and plan our approach now, rather than look back in eighteen years and regret a lack of direction and purpose. In order to take this proactive approach, we have worked hard to mesh our two lives and two different upbringings into a parenting philosophy that we can both agree upon. It has not been an easy road, but it has been one I'm glad we took.

The most effective tool for us was our desire to learn. We read books, asked questions, attended conferences, talked about our upbringing, and took several parenting classes. And we continue to do so as we enter into more uncharted waters of raising children. Along the way, we were introduced to the concept of family night. It was an idea that was new to both of us, but one we were drawn to. While we have not been successful in finding a consistent night during the week for family night, we take the time to plan for specific family evenings. Family nights never look exactly the same, but the results are consistent. With a little bit of creativity, we are closer, communicating better, and have the sense of being teammates on the same team.

One family I know designates Sunday night as family night. Mom and Dad refrain from committing to responsibilities in church or civic activities that require Sunday evening attendance and their older children know that they cannot accept activity invitations on Sunday evenings. This is because Sunday evenings are spent playing together as a family. Sometimes they play board games together while other times they leave the house to play miniature golf. The benefits of this time together are seen in increased communication and laughter, not to mention the special bonding their family experiences because of their priority of family activities.

I've talked with other families who value family nights. Here are some of their tips on family time:

- If possible set aside one night of the week that becomes sacred to your family. No one accepts an invitation that evening, no meetings, no social engagements—it's reserved for family night.

- If setting aside one night a week is not feasible with your family's schedule, sit down with the calendar and plan for some evenings together. Communicate to everyone these dates and keep them free from activities.
- Include the kids in planning the activities. Encourage their creativity. When they feel they have been valued in the planning process, their desire to participate increases.
- Don't be discouraged if the process of gathering everyone is met with frustration, especially early on. We all have a self-centered nature and have to be coached into understanding the importance of a team.
- Be creative with your evenings: game night (Scrabble, Monopoly, Pictionary), watching home movies, going through old photo albums, watching a movie together, baking cookies. Bowling, miniature golf, ice-skating, and even roller skating make for enjoyable family time, too.
- Don't doubt the ability to do family night just because your children are far apart in age. One summer we took the kids golfing (this was a "family morning") at the Par 3 course. The older children were able to golf while two-year-old Austin enjoyed the ride in the wagon we brought with us.

As parents, we have only one shot at raising our kids. It's not a job we can do over again. That's why creative activities that strengthen the family relationship are so important. I once heard author and speaker Gary Ezzo share, "Peer pressure is only as strong as family identity is weak." It's a statement that has stuck with me. Creative family nights are certainly one way we can develop family identity and further develop family relationships.

LET THE CREATIVE JUICES FLOW!

Creativity is not necessarily something you are born with. It is more about strategy than it is about being a creative person. It's not really about the ability to craft and create, but rather to think smart about time, finances, communication, relationships, and more! When it comes to mothering, let the creative juices flow by developing strategies, gathering resources, and implementing plans to achieve your goals!

──────────── A STEP FURTHER. . . ────────────

What creative communication do you use with your family? What activities or terms would you like to find some creative communication for? Brainstorm some ideas with your family.

❧

Determine three ways you can improve your time management by creatively using the minutes you have.

❧

What creative date could you and your husband do in the next week? Set up the sitter and make it happen today!

❧

Brainstorm with some friends about memorable and fun family night ideas. Share your ideas with each other and encourage one another to put the plans into action.

chapter 10

GRACE: IT HAS A PLACE IN YOUR HOME

I WAS LATE FOR A MEETING EARLY ONE MORNING. THE CHURCH MUSIC team met each Tuesday at 6 A.M. for prayer and planning, and I always had trouble arriving on time. Once again I had not left in enough time. I jumped into a car we had borrowed from my parents while one of our vehicles was being repaired. In rushing to get to the meeting on time, I exceeded the speed limit. As I approached the church, I noticed the red lights behind my car.

I pulled into the church parking lot and stopped. The officer approached the car and asked if I was aware that I had been traveling 45 mph in a 35 mph zone. I explained that I was in a hurry, and I was rushing rather than watching my speed.

He asked for my driver's license. I turned to get my purse and realized that in my hurry I had only grabbed my notebook. I had no driver's license in my possession. I apologized to him and explained that I must have left it at home in the hurry to get out the door.

He then asked for my vehicle registration papers. I searched everywhere I could think of to find the vehicle registration papers in my mother's car. I couldn't locate them anywhere. Once again I sheepishly turned to the officer and explained that I was borrowing my mother's car, and I couldn't find her registration papers. I explained that I was sure they were there somewhere. I just didn't know where.

By this time, I was prepared to have the book thrown at me. My thoughts tumbled one after the other. . . . *At the rate I'm going, this is going to cost a fortune in tickets. He could probably even take me in, if he wanted to. He could have the car towed and suspend my license. What have I done here?* I braced myself for the consequences that would be administered.

The officer paused for a moment and then said, "It's not worth it. Have a good day and please drive slower." He turned and got back in his car and drove away.

I stood next to my car, frozen with unbelief. I couldn't believe it. I deserved punishment. I should have had to suffer the consequences of my wrongdoings. But that officer determined to let it go. He acted as if it never happened. He offered me grace.

GRACE IS MORE THAN A MEALTIME PRAYER

Grace is a term our society is unfamiliar with. We hear a lot about justice, fairness, and legalities, but we don't often hear about grace. It is a term that God has used to describe His relationship with us. To better understand grace and how it fits into being a mother, we need to understand God's grace and the example He set for us.

God is perfect. We are not. When God extends grace to us He operates in a fashion similar to the police officer's except for one very big difference. Rather than saying, "It's not worth it," God says, "You are worth it." God continues by saying, "I know you make mistakes, but I love you unconditionally. My love is not based on your good deeds. In fact, it's not based upon anything you do at all. It's based upon who I am."

Webster's Dictionary defines grace as "the unmerited love and favor of God toward man." I love the word *unmerited* because I believe it explains grace very well. God's grace is extended to us even though we don't deserve it. It is undeserved. Unmerited. That is the beauty of grace.

Grace is a first cousin to forgiveness. Grace and forgiveness are very important tools for a mother to have in her toolbox. These tools help us to go the distance as wives and mothers. When we put these tools to work, we will see long-term positive responses in each family member's sense of self-worth, and we will find an unexplained peace in our own lives.

RESPOND OR REACT?

When family members make mistakes, we have two choices: we can inflict shame and guilt or we can respond with grace. Our words will reflect our heart and our heart will reflect our love. Is our love for others conditional, based on their actions, or unconditional, given freely and not based on good deeds?

God's love for us is unconditional and provides a perfect example of how we are to love others. No matter how much we mess up, how often we make poor choices, or how foolish we are, God still loves us. He responds with love.

When our children make mistakes, we will be the ones to either build them up with grace or tear them down with shame. When our spouse makes mistakes, we can either give words of life (grace) or words of death (shame). With this choice comes a powerful responsibility.

Ephesians 4:29 states, "Do not let any unwholesome talk come out of your mouths, but only what is helpful for building others up according to their needs, that it may benefit those who listen." Our words and our tone will reflect grace or shame. We must choose them wisely. Let's look at the two.

HEALTHY GUILT AND UNHEALTHY GUILT

God created the emotion of guilt for a very good reason. It accompanies the knowledge of doing something wrong. Our conscience equips us to process right and wrong, guilt and innocence. When we choose to do wrong we experience guilt, also known as conviction. Conviction produces in us a desire to change. If we don't feel convicted about our wrongdoing, we won't want to change and grow. Conviction is a very healthy and normal emotion.

Unfortunately, something that was created for good can also be taken to an extreme and become something unhealthy. We can feel so full of guilt and shame that we forget the unconditional love God has for us and come to believe that we're unlovable because of our wrong-doing. This is when guilt is overblown and turns into a destructive emotion known as condemnation.

Good guilt, or conviction, is from the Holy Spirit. It says, "That was a bad choice. I don't want to do that again." We are also reminded that we no longer have to make the same mistakes and that we can choose to live a better life when we partner with God. Conviction and the life change it brings about refreshes us!

Bad guilt, or condemnation, says, "That was a bad decision, and I am a bad person because I just can't get it right." Some might call this negative self-talk. I've heard it referred to as the audiotapes we play over and over again in our minds. We are so accustomed to the negative messages, we lose the ability to recognize them as the lies that they are. Condemnation cripples us as mothers. It causes us to believe the negative thoughts in our minds. It weighs us down, strips us of hope, and robs us of precious family time.

God's truth is the only weapon that can be used in the battle against condemnation. In Romans 8:1 we read, "Therefore, there is now no condemnation for those who are in Christ Jesus." God's plan is for us to operate within His unconditional love and grace. We are not worthless simply because we made a bad decision. God's love defines our worth and is not based upon our actions.

So why address something like grace and guilt in a book about motherhood? For two important reasons: our understanding of these concepts directly affects our family relationships, and there are a vast number of mothers who struggle with unhealthy shame.

My friend Shawn shared her struggles with condemnation as a mother in an article for her moms' group newsletter. Here's an excerpt of her story:

> [Earlier] I shared with you that I have often reflected on my life as a mother these last 13 years and have many times been disappointed with myself. I haven't always been loving, forgiving, caring, or selfless. Sadly, many times I have been just the opposite.

In those times, I remember feeling like the worst mother on the face of the planet. I would go to sleep at night on a tear-stained pillow, regretting my decisions. Regretting when I raised my voice, when I said no too frequently, when I did what I wanted to do instead of playing ball or watching them ride their bikes when they asked me to.

I would become lost in my grief to the point that I would continue to make wrong choices because I believed the lie that I was a bad mother. Have any of you been there?

... Jesus came to give us freedom from negative guilt. In its place He gives us hope, newness, and freedom! He believes in you and He believes in me! And He can certainly empower us to make good choices! And all the while, He stands right by us.

Which guilt dictates to you when you make mistakes in your mothering? Conviction or condemnation?

I believe Shawn's question is a good one. And I believe her experience with a mother's guilt is a common experience for many women. That is the reason I believe it is important for us to understand the tool of grace and how it is used in the profession of motherhood.

OUR HOME INTERNSHIP

In chapter 5, I introduced the term *home internship* in relation to our marriage. The idea is that primarily what we know about the marriage relationship comes from the home in which we grew up. We may have learned some very positive relationship skills or we may have had some relationally destructive behavior modeled for us. It is important that we evaluate our home internship to allow us to know both our strengths and weaknesses as spouses. Once we have identified the areas in which we are weak, we can pursue a new internship, doing whatever we can to relearn the concept in a healthy way.

The same idea applies to our understanding of grace and guilt. If we grew up in a home filled with grace, we will most often parent with grace and will readily accept God's grace. If we grew up in a home filled with shame, if love and affection were based upon good behavior, then we may find that we parent with guilt and struggle with condemnation.

It is important to evaluate our home as it relates to grace and guilt. We may need to relearn grace.

God wants to lead us through that relearning process. He has given us truth, in the Bible, to replace the lies or self-condemning behavior we are prone to. He has promised us that He will never leave us as we work through the process. And He has provided us with a perfect example of love, forgiveness, and grace. In the rest of this chapter we'll be developing new strategies for using the tool of grace in the profession of motherhood.

THE ROLE OF FORGIVENESS IN GRACE

Forgiveness is often a misunderstood term because we frequently categorize it as an emotion. Forgiveness is not an emotion at all—it is a choice. It is an action. It is an extension of grace from one person to another. Rather than shaming and ridiculing others, we can choose to forgive them for their mistakes and, in so doing, offer them grace.

Offering grace to others is deciding to let the wrong be a part of the past. In recognizing our inadequacies, we can also allow others something we might call "grace space." Grace space is the act of allowing others to be different from ourselves, recognizing the unique way that God has wired each one of us, rather than trying to change others to be like us. When we allow grace space, we are affirming others in their gifts and talents, bringing out the best in people, and building others up as we accept our differences.

Can you imagine how many marriages might be changed if we all understood grace space? Can you imagine how many children would grow up knowing they are valued for who they are if we each operated by allowing grace space? The ramifications of putting this concept into action could be world changing!

CONTROL AND GRACE: CAN THE TWO EXIST TOGETHER?

I sat and listened as my friend—I'll call her Janna—poured out her heart. She was so unhappy with the wife and the mother she had become, and she truly wanted to make some changes—she just didn't know where to begin. Her mother had always had high expectations of her. She would manipulate behavior by withholding love and affection. She acted ashamed when her children would misbehave. Her love and acceptance felt very conditional to her children.

Janna's mother had operated with the same damaging strategy in her marriage. She manipulated her spouse using rage or the silent treatment. She did whatever was necessary to control the people around her.

Now my friend is finding herself reacting to her children and husband in a similar way. She doesn't like what is happening, but this is the behavior she learned in her home internship. She handles misbehavior with shaming statements. She rages to regain control in the midst of disagreement or disorder. When it comes to her relationship with her husband, she has become an expert in nonverbal communication. The silent treatment and withholding sex are her two most used methods of managing marital conflict.

This kind of shaming, guilt-laying reaction to other people has a name—control. Some of us have a high desire to control the actions and behaviors of others. For those of us in the profession of motherhood, this desire is most often seen in our relationships with our children and our husbands.

Left unchecked, this type of reaction to other family members can cause deep damage to the relationships involved and to the self-worth of those who are victims of the control. We're not talking about an occasional "losing it with the kids." We're talking about negative and shaming messages that are the primary way of communicating with a spouse or with children.

Jeff VanVonderen explains this unhealthy shaming pattern in his book *Families Where Grace Is in Place*. He states that shame-based family relationships have the following characteristics:

1. *Verbal shaming*: Spoken or insinuated messages of "What's wrong with you?", "Why can't you be like. . . ?"
2. *Performance-orientation*: Good behavior gains acceptance and approval.
3. *Unspoken rules*: Behavior is governed by rules that are seldom stated. Sometimes the only way to find out about the rule is when it is broken.

4. *Communication through coding*: This often happens when family members send messages in either nonverbal communication or through other family members.

5. *Idolatry*: How things look, what people think, what possessions are owned are most important.

6. *Putting kids through a hard time*: Because how things look is so important, children must learn to act like miniature adults in order to avoid shame.

7. *Preoccupation with fault and blame*: When humiliation has been brought to the family because of the misbehavior of a family member, fault and blame are top priorities. This way the "problem" person can be shamed, humiliated, and made to feel so bad that he won't do the behavior again.

8. *Strong on "head skills"*: Blaming, rationalizing, minimizing, and denial are used to defend oneself.

9. *Weak on "heart skills"*: Feelings are wrong, selfish, or unnecessary.

10. *Needy people*: Family members are empty on the inside, but look good on the outside.[10]

Jeff makes a powerful statement that I think explains very well the dilemma we have as mothers and wives who want to control. He says, "God's job is to fix and to change. Our job is to depend [on God], serve, and equip. This is the work of grace. And it is more restful than you can imagine."[11]

My friend Janna was absolutely exhausted from trying to control everyone and everything around her, and she was seeing the futility of her efforts. She wanted to learn a different way to respond to her husband and her children. She also recognized the damage she had done to friendships with this controlling behavior and wanted to see that change, too. The place Janna has to start, and the place you and I have to start, is with grace. When we're controlling, we're taking on a job that we're not designed to do. That is God's job. When we operate with grace, we are able to do what God asks us to do and leave the "fixing and changing" stuff to God.

Jeff VanVonderen goes on to explain the traits of relationships that are filled with grace. They are focused on building people up rather than trying to fix people. Here are ten characteristics that describe grace-filled relationships, which produce competence, creativity, and contentment in people.

1. *Verbal affirming*: Family members are told they are capable, valuable, accepted, and supported. Most importantly they are told they are loved.

2. *People-oriented*: Love and acceptance does not fluctuate depending on how people act. People are affirmed for who they are, not just for how they act.

3. *Out-loud rules and expectations*: Rather than unspoken rules, rules are stated and are there to serve the people; people aren't there to serve the rules.

4. *Communication is clear and straight*: Messages are communicated with words, not hints; honest feedback is given. Example: If you want someone to take out the garbage, ask them to do so. Don't say, "It sure would be nice if someone would take out the garbage."

5. *God is the source*: Our sense of well-being and value come from God, not from the behavior of another person.

6. *Children are enjoyed*: Kids can be kids rather than little adults who can't mess up. Example: As parents, we don't need to be threatened or take it personally when our children mess up. They aren't broken, and we don't have to fix them. They are simply exploring life, finding out what's real.

7. *Responsibility and accountability*: Rather than using fault and blame for punishing and controlling wrong behavior, people are responsible for their choices and it is appropriate to hold them accountable for them.

8. *"Head skills" are used for learning:* Rather than using head skills for defending, thinking is used for the purpose of learning.

9. *Feelings are valid and useful*: Grace-filled families recognize the feeling and expression of emotions as opportunities for family members to connect, to restore relationships, or to

support one another in making wise choices in response to how we feel.

10. *It's OK for outsides to match insides*: Rather than putting on a front, grace-filled families are concerned with how people really are; what is real is more important than how things look.[12]

As mothers it is so important that we understand the tool of grace and its use in our profession. Our words and our attitudes are incredibly powerful and can have long-lasting effects upon our families. If you struggle with control, grace is the place to begin.

Don't shame yourself if you identify more with the characteristics of shame-based family relationships. Use this as an opportunity to understand the tool of grace and begin to make positive changes. Use the characteristics of grace-filled families to assist you in setting goals for yourself.

To understand grace, we must begin by understanding our value in God's eyes. VanVonderen states, "If our sense of well-being and value come from the behavior of another person instead of God, we will always be giving off messages that say to others: You'd better perform right."[13]

As mothers, our self-worth has to come from our value in God, not from the behavior of our children or the actions of our husbands. Additionally, we must understand how being grace-filled wives and mothers can empower our husbands and children.

A GRACE-FILLED MARRIAGE

For the past seven years, Mark and I have made ourselves available to mentor couples who are struggling in their marriages. We have spent time with literally hundreds of couples who were in a variety of marital stages: some struggling with smaller daily issues; others who were on the verge of divorce. In most of these relationships, a lack of grace was a major component of the frustration or even disaster they were experiencing in their marriages.

After the honeymoon is over, we begin to see the real way our spouses act and live. When children are added to the family, we now have less time for one another and the little things begin to bother us.

What eventually happens is that both partners become experts at identifying what their spouses do wrong. If grace is not in place, shame, guilt, and condemnation will happen instead.

When Mark and I were at the height of our struggles, condemnation was one of our primary issues. I find that many wives struggle with this. Indeed, many times we are very quick to tell our husbands what they do not do well. When we fall into this pit of condemnation, affirmation ceases to exist. I have talked to far too many husbands who feel that they can't do anything right when it comes to their wives. They simply can't measure up. This happens when shame becomes the controlling communication rather than grace. Shame makes people feel they can't measure up, whereas grace builds people up.

Several years ago, our family drove from our home in central Illinois to visit friends and family in Colorado. With four children in tow, the youngest less than two years old, this trip was incredibly trying at times. All in all, the kids traveled well, but on the way home, as we crossed from Iowa to Illinois on Interstate 80, both Mark and I were really looking forward to the trip being over.

Austin became a bit fussy, so I moved to the back of the van to try to entertain him for a while. I had probably been in the back about an hour when I finally moved to the front seat of the van again. As I buckled my seat belt, I noticed a sign stating that we were on Interstate 80 nearing Morris, Illinois. I knew immediately this was not right. We were supposed to be on Interstate 74 and we should be nearing Peoria about this time. After Peoria, we would have only a forty-minute drive home. Morris is considered a Chicago suburb. We were not supposed to be near Chicago. Morris, Illinois is a good two hours from our home in Bloomington, Illinois.

Mark was tired. We had been driving for two days. He missed the Interstate 74 connection shortly after we crossed into Illinois. I was busy keeping Austin happy at just the time it would have been a benefit to have two sets of eyes watching the road.

I'm sorry to report that I chose to react with shame and anger at my husband. I could have responded with grace, but I didn't. Yes, I was disappointed and angry. But I had a choice to either respond with grace or react with shame. Unfortunately, I made the wrong choice.

Our vacation was now marred by my inappropriate tone and words. My husband was hurt. My children were hurt. I had to repair the damage by asking for forgiveness and apologizing for my actions. I'm afraid this scene was a perfect illustration for the ten characteristics of shame-based relationships. It was also a turning point for me to realize how often my tone, words, or actions were shame-based and how I needed to make a change for myself and my family.

Let me share another story. This one has a different ending.

My friend Doris was traveling with her husband and son from their home in Illinois to a family wedding in Nashville, Tennessee. Doris was driving as their son, Hunter, slept in the backseat. Her husband, Charlie, was doing some work on the laptop computer in the passenger seat. Their family was preparing to relocate from Illinois to Florida, and as Doris drove, she was mentally making a list of all the tasks she needed to do for their move. After quite an extensive time of driving, Doris began to wonder when they were going to hit the Kentucky border. It seemed like it was taking an awfully long time to cross the Ohio River. Finally, she saw the bridge ahead. As they approached the bridge, Doris noticed a sign that read "Mississippi River." After crossing the bridge, she spotted a "Welcome to Missouri" sign. She realized immediately that she must have missed an exit somewhere. She began to panic.

Charlie had been busy on the computer and had not even noticed a change in scenery. Upon Doris's proclamation that they had crossed the Mississippi River into Missouri, Charlie reached for the map. He saw the place where the highway had split and Doris had mistakenly missed the intended interstate. He began to give her directions to get them back on track to their Tennessee wedding. The mistake cost them about two hours travel time.

Shortly after the trip, Doris shared this story with me. She was now able to laugh at herself and the little tour of Missouri that they took on their way to Tennessee. But what impacted her most was the way Charlie handled the situation with grace. That is what impacted me most, too. He could have shamed her, he could have told her how foolish she was, and he could have never let her forget it. But he didn't. He operated with grace and forgiveness. His response was encouraging rather than discouraging. He realized that we all make mistakes and we all deserve unmerited favor in our relationships.

Because of his response, Charlie had no mending to do. No one was hurt. Doris continued driving with her dignity in place. Their family made it to Tennessee and enjoyed a wonderful wedding. That is the power of grace.

GRACE-FILLED PARENTING

Grace is a tool that needs to be used daily in our parenting. It builds up our children. It gives them permission to be different. It allows them to make mistakes.

At the same time, grace should not be confused with permissiveness. Grace simply represents an attitude that we need to use, even in the midst of correction. Children need to be held accountable for their choices, and they need to be empowered to make good choices. Grace doesn't mean we look the other way when they are disobedient. It means we handle the situation without shaming, ridiculing, or blaming.

All of us, both children and adults, need to understand there are consequences for our choices. We are responsible for the decisions we make. As parents, we need to teach our children about this responsibility. When they make mistakes, we need to assist them in learning from the mistake. Sometimes that may happen just by talking to them about it and sometimes it may happen by experiencing a consequence.

Several years ago I heard a Christian song that made a powerful impact on me. The title was "You're the Only Jesus Some Will Ever See." I have often thought of that phrase in the midst of my mothering. For our children, we represent Jesus. We're the only Jesus they see now. Because of that, we need to represent God's character to them inasmuch as it is humanly possible. Our relationship with God is based on grace; therefore, our relationship with our children should have the same foundation.

In the midst of teaching and training our children, grace needs to be the primary tool used. Grace is expressed in unconditional love, out-loud affirming, clear and straight communication, valued feelings and emotions, and the freedom for outsides to match insides. When we operate as parents with these traits of grace, we nurture our children to develop into competent and emotionally healthy adults.

GRACE IS WHAT IT TAKES

I am amazed at the steep learning curve that I have had since I entered the profession of motherhood. Although my home internship was a very positive experience, there are still so many things I simply could not understand and could not apply until I was in the midst of motherhood.

For me, grace was one of those concepts I never understood before and am striving to implement in my marriage and my family. I know I have made huge strides over the years, but I still have growing to do in this area.

I know I want my husband to feel our home is a bit of a haven, a place to find rest, affirmation, and encouragement. Grace is what will make that happen. I know I want my children to live in a home that encourages individuality, competency, and contentment. Grace is what it will take.

That police officer offered me grace. God offers all of us grace. Let us continue the process and give grace a place in our homes.

———— A STEP FURTHER. . . ————

What was your home internship like as it pertains to grace? Was grace prevalent or was shame used more often? How has that experience affected your parenting?

෨෨

Identify three ways you can give "grace space" to your husband.

Identify three ways you can give "grace space" to your children.

∽

If condemnation is something you struggle with, take a few minutes to ask God to help identify the lies that come your way and to replace them with God's truth.

chapter 11

HUMOR: LET'S LAUGH A BIT!

THE RULES OF CHOCOLATE

- If you've got melted chocolate all over your hands, you're eating it too slowly.
- Chocolate-covered raisins, cherries, orange slices, and strawberries all count as fruit, so eat as many as you want.
- The problem: How do you get two pounds of chocolate home from the store in a hot car?
  The solution: Eat it in the parking lot.
- Diet tip: Eat a chocolate bar before each meal. It'll take the edge off your appetite, and you'll eat less.
- A nice box of chocolates can provide your total daily intake of calories in one place. Isn't that handy?
- Q: Why is there no such organization as Chocoholics Anonymous?
  A: Because no one wants to quit.
- Put "eat chocolate" at the top of your list of things to do today. That way, at least you'll get one thing done!

Did the above make you smile? I hope it brought a grin to your face and even made you laugh a little. If it didn't, then either you really do need to lighten up or you are like my friend Becky and you don't like chocolate. Truly, I can't imagine life without chocolate. I love it so much that I served M&M's at my wedding! Although I could probably write an entire chapter to support the premise that chocolate is a necessary tool for the profession of motherhood, I think I'll let that one go and stick with humor.

Humor is good for us both emotionally and physically. God created laughter, and it's part of His plan for us to live happy lives. We must let ourselves laugh and be willing to laugh at ourselves. It is a vital tool for the profession of motherhood.

One of the most well-liked speakers at Hearts at Home conferences has been author and speaker Becky Freeman. Becky tells stories about real life at the Freeman home. She's not afraid to share even the most personal, foolish mistakes she has made. Women can identify with her, and they laugh. And laugh. And laugh. And laugh. She makes you laugh so hard that your stomach hurts, your cheeks ache, and tears roll down your face.

Our evaluations always ring in a positive response to Becky as a speaker. The attendees comment about how good it felt to laugh. "Becky helped me laugh again." "I haven't laughed that hard in a long time." "Wow! I feel refreshed as a mother, just being able to laugh like we did!" It is good to laugh, and we do need to do it more often.

I asked in chapter 7: *When did we forget how to play?* I'll ask now: *When did we forget how to laugh?* The average child laughs hundreds of times a day. The average adult laughs only a dozen times.

When did we start taking life *so* seriously that we left behind our sense of humor or our ability to laugh at ourselves? When did we forget the power of a smile?

The medical benefits of laughter are incredible. Laughter can lower blood pressure, increase muscle flexion, and trigger a flood of endorphins—the brain chemicals that can bring on euphoria. Laughter profoundly affects our immune systems. Gamma-interferon, a disease-fighting protein, rises with laughter. So do B-cells, which produce disease-destroying antibodies, and T-cells, which orchestrate our body's immune response. Laughter can also shut off the flow of stress hormones—the fight-or-flight compounds that come into play when we feel hostility, rage, and stress. Stress hormones suppress the immune system, raise blood pressure, and increase the number of platelets in our blood, which can cause fatal artery blockages.[14] Obviously, laughter is not just valuable to our mental and emotional health, it is important to our physical health.

THE HUMOR PERSPECTIVE

David Burke is a gifted writer who often contributes to the *Hearts at Home* magazine, produced monthly by Hearts at Home. One article David wrote was entitled "Children Are Anarchists." To be honest, I wasn't sure exactly what the word *anarchist* meant. I looked it up, and *Webster's Dictionary* explained that an anarchist is someone who causes disorder. I'd have to say that I do believe this term describes children well. Life with children is anarchy, a state of disorder, which is why it is so important that we learn to laugh. Things rarely go the way we expect them to.

I asked David if he would allow me to share his thoughts with you, and he agreed. I hope you enjoy this as much as I did.

CHILDREN ARE ANARCHISTS

by David Burke

They are the unstackers of the folded; the diggers up of the freshly planted; the wakers of the sleeping.

They are the spillers of what they shouldn't have; the breakers of what they've been told not to touch; the wielders of permanent markers around all-white surfaces.

They are a testament to the Second Law of Thermodynamics: Everything proceeds from order to ever-increasing disorder, until ultimately the universe becomes unhinged.

I have watched my youngest put her brother's sneaker in the microwave and press "on" with no more hesitation than a hungry homemaker preparing an eight-minute Chicken Kiev.

I've witnessed my middle son stencil his initials into the carpet with crayon, in front of God and grandparents, then express genuine surprise that anybody's upset.

I've seen my oldest son balance precariously on a footstool at the top of the stairs, naked from the waist down, reaching for a balloon, and realize that he interrupted a trip to the bathroom to do it.

I've watched all three, unprompted and unsupervised, wash my car. Did I mention my windows were down at the time?

Children are the scatterers of the 700-piece Lego set; the misplacers of the puzzle corner pieces; the announcers that they have to go to the bathroom in an otherwise quiet church service.

They are a living variation on Murphy's Law: "If anything can go wrong, well—you probably should have known better than to leave the kids in the same room with the cat and the hair gel."

Life among the anarchists means learning never to be surprised, a lesson we got when our oldest son stacked every toy, Tupperware dish, article of clothing, piece of furniture, and sleeping pet in the middle of the living room and insisted we call him "the garbage man."

Yet, even knowing all this, we continue to a) procreate, and b) unleash our kids on an unsuspecting world. Consider the events of December 20, 1996, for example, during the annual Good Shepherd Preschool Christmas Pageant: One of my children arrived at the manger scene late, minus his costume, "bonking" two of his buddies with a shepherd's crook, which effectively turned the Nativity Scene into a Three Stooges Revival. ("Let us go unto Bethlehem and see what the Lord has made known to us—nyuk, nyuk, nyuk.")

And, despite overwhelming evidence to the contrary, we continue to put them in the most structured of all events—the wedding ceremony—and insist we can control the outcome.

Imagine my surprise a few years ago when my then three-year-old son was asked to be ring bearer in a family wedding.

Consider my alarm when, despite several months of protests, both of us ended up at the front of the church as part of the wedding party.

There we stood in our matching tuxedos, me sweating with eyes darting about nervously, he gnawing on the wooden altar rail behind me. When he turned his attention to the church piano legs, I decided it was time to drop all pretense of proto-col and scooped him up.

In a mental file I've labeled, "Life's Stupidest Moments," I'll forever remember my son flailing like a rabid beaver in my out-stretched arms, screaming "NO" at the top of his lungs, and then, with the callous efficiency of a Mafia hit man, whacking me on top of the head with his ring bearer's pillow, the symbol of love and unity.

As I put my son down and finger-combed the red-velvet lint out of my hair, a wave of laughter began to swell from the back of the room. By the time it crested over the first pew, I was still distracted, wondering if anyone caught the moment on video-tape and how much it would be worth on "America's Funniest Home Videos." When it spilled over onto the wedding party, though, I saw the moment in my head the way they must have, and soon I, too, was laughing.

Phyllis Diller once said that, "Cleaning your house [and, presumably, maintaining any other semblance of a normal life] while children are growing is like shoveling your driveway while it's still snowing." The anarchy of parenthood is inevitable, and trying too hard to resist it will probably only net you a slow descent into madness.

And you could miss some good stuff in the process. I've been around enough reminiscing grandparents to know that it's the chaotic moments with our children that we'll probably remem-ber most fondly later (maybe that's why they're always giving my kids candy when I'm not looking).

So, like that day in my ill-fitting tuxedo, the impression of crushed velvet minted into my hair and forehead, I hope I'll spend a little less time trying to contain what's going on around me and a little more time laughing at the results.

And I'll keep the camcorder rolling—I could use the money.[15]

I love David's statement in the last paragraph, "I hope I'll spend a little less time trying to contain what's going on around me and a little more time laughing at the results." That is the key to the tool of humor. If we keep trying to control the world around us, we will miss so many opportunities to just enjoy them and laugh about them for years to come.

HUMOR HANG-UPS

Humor is an opportunity to lighten up our world. It helps us process life. It helps us manage relationships. Sometimes, though, we can't seem to find the humor button. We don't find anything funny. We are stuck in serious mode and don't know how to get out. Or perhaps we are stuck in anger mode and can't find our way to humor.

My dear friend Charlene Baumbich is a pro at finding the funny side of life. Many times she has encouraged women at Hearts at Home conferences with her workshop entitled, "Humor—Mom's Secret Weapon." During her workshop she shares what she calls "Humor Hog-ties," things that get in the way of humor in our life. Let me share with you what I call Humor Hang-ups. The first four are from Charlene's Humor Hog-tie list and the rest are a few of my own.

Humor Hang-up #1—*Busyness*: Doing too much and being in a hurry keeps us from letting humor play a role in our hearts.

Humor Hang-up #2—*Making Something That Should Be Joy-filled a Stressor*: When we let the responsibilities of a project outweigh the joys. It's also when we try to make something more complicated than it needs to be.

Humor Hang-up #3—*Too Much Importance Given to What Isn't Important*: Getting upset about something that truly won't matter ten years from now. Have you ever argued with a child over something that simply isn't important? Why do we let such little things bog us down?

Humor Hang-up #4—*Fear that the person you are mad at will no longer be punished by your anger*: Letting anger rule your heart rather than grace or forgiveness. Now really, when we use anger to punish someone, who is really punished? We are, and it is a waste of our energies.

Humor Hang-up #5—*Expectations set too high*: If we don't accept that life with children will include disorder, we will always be frustrated because we feel out of control. We can become obsessed with unrealistic expectations and allow them to steal our joy.

Humor Hang-up #6—*Forgot how to have fun*: Believing that now that you are an adult you can't be silly anymore. Even as adults, we can still have slumber parties with our girlfriends, Chinese fire drills (ask my friend Nancy about that one!), Silly String wars, and pillow fights.

Do you have any humor hang-ups in your life? It's never too late to make changes and to approach life with a different strategy. Don't let hang-ups rob the joy God has given you.

JOYFUL MOMENTS

God's plan for us is to have joy. Throughout the Bible we find verse after verse about joy. In John 15:11, God shares about His love for us and then says, "I have told you this so that my joy may be in you and that your joy may be complete." God takes joy in us, even when we mess up the perfect plan He has for us. In the same way, we can take joy in our children, even when they mess up the perfect plan we have for them.

God has given us the emotion of joy, which produces smiles, humor, and laughter. It's no coincidence that laughter produces the physical effects I mentioned earlier in this chapter. God created our bodies and gave us our emotions to work in conjunction with our bodies. Joy plays a specific role both emotionally and physically according to God's perfect design. Our goal as mothers is to learn how to find joy and humor in the daily moments of life.

Charlene Baumbich's sons are now adults. When she speaks to mothers, she shares from a "been there, done that" perspective that gives each listener hope for the future and a lighthearted view of the past. Charlene shares a story about the challenges of potty training one of her two sons. She was convinced his future wife was going to have to change his diapers. All of the women always laugh at this comment, and then Charlene asks them, "Why is that funny?" I love the statement she makes after that, "Do we laugh because when we exaggerate some thought enough, it might help us understand its lack of importance for the moment?"

I think Charlene makes a key point with that question. A little bit of whimsical imagination (thinking of this child as an adult wearing diapers) helps us lighten up for the moment and even laugh at the situation. As mothers, we need to use the tool of laughter regularly during this child-rearing season of life. If not, we will miss the magical, joyful moments God gives us when life doesn't go exactly as we planned it.

THE ROLE OF SPONTANEITY

Life with children is a life that is destined not to go as planned. The very first time I was introduced to that idea was when I was overdue with our first child. My due date came and went, much to my dismay. By the time I was nearing two weeks late, I waddled into my weekly OB/GYN appointment. As the doctor examined me I could tell he was troubled. I'll never forget his words, "Jill, this baby is sitting feet first. It's your first baby. You are two weeks overdue. I don't believe it's in your best interest or the baby's best interest to allow you to go into labor with a double, footling breech baby. I'd like to schedule a cesarean tomorrow morning."

I remember driving home from that appointment with tears streaming down my face. *This isn't the way it was supposed to happen. I don't want to have a cesarean. I didn't even pay attention during the childbirth classes when they talked about a cesarean section because I didn't think it applied to me!"* My perfect plans for this perfect birth were quickly unraveling. Life was not going as I had planned.

Little did I realize that this was only a preview of what was yet to come. Oh, the situations weren't all as big as a cesarean section, but they still had the ability to shipwreck the best-laid plans. You know those times. It's when you have everything packed and ready to walk out the door on a cold, wintery day. The baby has his snowsuit on and is wrapped in a blanket. As you pick him up you hear that unmistakable sound—yes, he's filling his diaper. You weigh your options: (A) change the child when we arrive at our destination thirty miles away, or (B) do the job now. You know you can't leave the poor thing in a dirty diaper for a thirty-mile trip, so you choose option B.

That's not all, though. As you remove the blanket and snowsuit you realize this child did not just fill his diaper—he filled his entire outfit. You are now faced with more than a diaper change, but a clothing change and even a possible bath.

Talk about things not going as planned. This is where we have a choice. There is a fork in the road. We can react with anger or we can respond with grace and, yes, even humor. Learning to respond with grace and humor is an act of replacing well-thought-out plans with a bit of spontaneity.

Author and speaker Susan Alexander Yates shares a story about a time when her children were small. One of her older children had a sporting event to attend, and they were rushing to get out the door. In the midst of this chaotic moment, Susan couldn't locate her twins, who were preschoolers at the time. They searched high and low until Susan finally found them playing very quietly in a secluded spot in the house. In their possession was a tube of Desitin cream. Giggling and laughing, without a care in the world, they had removed their clothes and were smearing the cream all over each other.

This was certainly not the plan that Susan had for her children that day. She faced that fork in the road and chose to handle it with grace and humor. She quickly put some clothes on these two sticky, white children and put them in the car. Any further delay would have caused them to miss the older sibling's game. Susan shares that throughout the game the kids tumbled and played in the grass and, by the time they headed home, they had twigs and leaves sticking to every part of their bodies.

Susan's value as a mother didn't change because of the appearance of these two children. Her value isn't based upon the behavior or actions of her children. Her value is based in Jesus Christ, and that never changes. Keeping that in mind allows us to have our perfect plans rocked sometimes. It helps us maintain perspective. It permits us to change from our planned expectations to the spontaneity of the moment. And sometimes it even helps us to learn to laugh at ourselves.

LIGHTEN UP

Renee is a busy mother of three. Her oldest is school age while the youngest is just under a year. One afternoon she headed out to do her after-school carpooling. She arrived early enough to be right near the front of the line of cars. As she summed up the wait ahead of her, she decided to just close her eyes and rest a minute. It had been a long day, and she hadn't sat down at all. The next thing she remembered was waking up and seeing the cars that were behind her slowly moving around her. She had fallen fast asleep for those few minutes, completely unaware that school was out and the carpool line was moving. And all those other nice mothers knew how incredibly tired this poor mom was, so they just let her sleep and drove right around her.

Renee and her sister, Michele, laughed and laughed about that situation as Renee shared it. The incident was embarrassing for Renee, but after she moved past the shock of it, she decided to offer herself some grace. Sometimes we just need to laugh at ourselves.

Sharing our stories is cathartic. When we share our stories we may first be stewing about it, or terribly embarrassed, but when we hear ourselves tell the story and hear others laugh about the situation, we can then see the humor in it and begin to change our perspective.

We're all human. We will make mistakes. We will say the wrong thing. We will do the wrong thing. We will embarrass ourselves. When these things happen, and they will, we need to pull out the tool of humor and use it to its fullest.

Like my friend David said, "The anarchy of parenthood is inevitable, and trying too hard to resist it will probably only net you a slow descent into madness." If we don't learn to laugh at ourselves and our circumstances, we will drive ourselves crazy. God gave us joy for a reason. Let's use it to its fullest!

─────────── A STEP FURTHER. . . ───────────

What can you do to increase your response of humor to life's frustrating or embarrassing situations?

෬

What humor hang-up can you identify with the most? Why?

෬

How is your level of spontaneity? Expect the unexpected is a common theme of full-time motherhood. In what areas of life do you need to adjust your expectations to better handle the unexpected?

෬

Remember three instances that at the time were stressful but in retrospect are amusing. Share them with a friend and enjoy a good laugh together.

chapter 12

ORGANIZATION:
I CAN'T GO ANYWHERE
WITHOUT MY PLANNER!

I LOGGED ON MY COMPUTER AND PICKED UP MY EMAIL. I NOTICED THERE was a message from Karla, the worship director at the small church where my husband was serving as an interim pastor. "Jill, we missed you at choir last night. I hope everything is OK. Karla." I panicked for a brief moment. Was last night Wednesday night? (Stay-at-home mother dilemma #368: Sometimes you can't remember what day of the week it is!) How did I manage to forget choir? I wasn't just a choir member, believe it or not, I was serving as the director for a short season of time! How could I forget choir? I ran into the dining room and grabbed my calendar. I looked and found that, sure enough, I did not write choir practice on the calendar for the previous evening. I looked at the preceding two Wednesdays and found where I had noted choir practice on those dates, but for some reason I had not written it on the calendar past the first two weeks.

I don't know about you, but my ability to keep the details of life straight is dependent on the availability of pencil and paper. And personally, I don't know where I would be in life without sticky notes. I stick them all over the place—mirrors, telephone, computer, notebooks, desks. I use them in the house, in the car, and even carry them in my purse. I've heard you lose brain cells every time you have a baby. I do believe most of my lost cells were in the area of memory. Additionally, with all the schedules of every individual family member it really would be physically impossible to remember all the details without some help.

In the past decade, day planners have rapidly become essential for many people. Daytimers, Franklin Planners, and Palm Pilots lead the way in the world of organizers. Most of those products are geared to assist the person working in the business world. In fact, many moms who have made the transition from careers in the business world to the profession of motherhood are quite adept at using these tools.

Technology and all of its benefits are not simply for those in the business world. Women in the profession of motherhood need a method for organizing time, information, and family details. A planner is an excellent management tool to assist in keeping Mom on top of all the family activities. It gathers pertinent information into one place. It helps keep tasks and projects organized. It is a tool that assists us with keeping many of life's details at our fingertips.

With all the organizing tools available, it is important to give thought to the particular needs you have in organizing time, resources, and schedules. The options are endless and the individual needs of each mother vary greatly. Let's look at our options and consider the need for an organizational tool.

WHERE DO I START?

The selection of a planner is very much a personal choice. What works for one person may not work for another. Initially, you must determine if you want a notebook-style planner or an electronic planner. I find that using both works well for me.

A notebook planner allows for very flexible use as the need arises. Do you need a place to keep notes from the Sunday sermon? Make a section in your notebook. Do you need a place to keep project notes when you are redecorating one of the kids' bedrooms? Dedicate a spot in your notebook to keep the prices, measurements, and paint samples together. The flexibility of the notebook planner is probably its biggest asset.

An electronic planner allows for information to be compacted in a small, sleek instrument that fits easily in a pocket or purse. The ability to carry most of your information with you without a bulky notebook is very helpful. The downfall of an electronic planner is the lack of flexibility. Many electronic planners have a place for notes, but they don't allow for lengthy note taking.

I find that using both an electronic planner and a notebook planner works well for me. I prefer to keep my calendar (appointments, meetings, kids' activity schedule, etc.) in my electronic planner. I love being able to schedule follow-up doctor or orthodontist appointments with my calendar in tow. Before I had an electronic calendar, I'd make appointments only to go home and check the family calendar and find that the date I scheduled wouldn't work for one reason or another. I do also keep a family calendar at home in the kitchen. Everyone in the family is responsible for writing their activities on the calendar to keep family members apprised of schedules and activities. Every Sunday evening I take a few minutes to check and make sure my electronic calendar and the family calendar match.

I also keep phone numbers and addresses in my electronic calendar. This helps when traveling and even just running around town. If I remember that I need to call the kids' school while I'm running errands, I have the number with me and can easily make the call from my cell phone or a pay phone. An electronic planner doesn't have to be terribly expensive. I found mine at the local electronics store for less than $100. Because we rarely have an extra $100 lying around, I waited and purchased mine with some birthday money.

I keep a notebook planner for just about everything else. Shopping lists, gift ideas, kids' immunization records, "to do" lists, and project details are just a few of the things in my three-ring notebook planner. It's a great help to know where the information is when needed.

When it comes to selecting a notebook planner there are two options: use a brand-name planner or create one yourself. Either way, you will need to determine size. Do you prefer an 8½" x 11", a 6" x 9", or a pocket-size planner? If you want to be able to insert meeting handouts or information sent home from school, an 8½" x 11" size would be a good choice. If you want to be able to easily carry it with you, the 6" x 9" or pocket size might be better.

When contemplating your organizational needs, take an inventory of what information you would like to put your fingers on quickly. Here are some things to consider:

- *Calendar*: Everybody uses different kinds of calendars. Some prefer a day at a glance, some a week at a glance, and others a month at a glance. Determine which you prefer and find a calendar that works best for you. Mark and I compare our calendars each month. He makes sure I'm aware of any evening meetings he might have and I alert him to school concerts, sports schedules, and extra music lessons.

- *Birthday List*: Keeping a list of birthdays and anniversaries for friends, family, and other significant relationships is helpful. Each January the list can be used to note the birthdays on the new year calendar.

- *Goals*: Setting annual goals is a good habit to get into. Spiritual goals, physical goals, marriage goals, and personal goals are all good to consider. Setting goals for each child can be helpful, too, as you consider his or her age and the concepts you would like to see him or her understand.

- *Lists*: Three important lists to keep are "To Do," "To Buy," and "To Call." These keep you reminded of the tasks to be accomplished. Don't forget to adjust your "to do" list to include the things you are really accomplishing as a mother (see Chapter 2). Additional lists can be helpful such as Camping Supplies and a Travel Packing List if your family camps or travels a lot.

- *Family Member Information*: Keep social security numbers of family members, clothing needs, and gift ideas all in one place. I can't tell you how many times I've needed to refer to the kids' social security numbers as they have grown older. I've managed to memorize my number and my husband's num-

number, but I couldn't possibly remember four more nine-digit numbers!

- *Medical Information*: A page on each child including immunizations, medication allergies, medical history, dates of annual physicals and dentist appointments. I used this section to track multiple allergic reactions to antibiotics for our daughter Anne. Over a span of several years, we found that she could only tolerate one antibiotic in all the different families of antibiotics. By having a place to track this I had the information at my fingertips when needed. It especially came in handy when she had to have an emergency appendectomy several years ago. As they prepared to take her in I met with the doctor and briefed him on her history. He wanted to know what medicines she had been given and what reaction followed. My documentation helped to provide fast and accurate information to get her the best medical care.

- *Menu Planner*: This section can help Mom strategically plan meals based upon family activities, food on hand, and extra guests. Thinking ahead about meals can assist in shopping, budgeting, and preparation. I also keep a list of favorite creative snacks to fix for the kids after school. Sometimes I get in a rut and just need to be reminded of my options. Keeping a list of favorite side dishes, desserts, and recipes also helps in meal planning. Sometimes a glance at the list is all it takes to remind me of something I haven't prepared in a while!

- *Grocery Planner*: This can be a preprinted shopping list with a place to list additional items and other errands to run. Items that need to be returned can also be noted so they are not forgotten.

- *Ideas*: This is a great place to jot down notes or draw a picture of a craft or gift idea seen in a store or someone else's home. If I'm at someone's home and see what a great job they did sponge painting their dining room, I can jot down the information they give me and their name and number for future reference should I decide to do the same.

- *Projects*: This is a great place to keep notes about redecorating projects, gardening ideas, or Christmas party details.
- *Responsibilities*: Year-round volunteer responsibilities such as teaching Sunday school, helping with story hour at the public library, or delivering Meals On Wheels can come with schedules, notes, and contact names and numbers. This is a good place to keep these items.
- *School*: Home-schooling moms can use this type of section for field trip contacts and ideas, goals for kids, and even assignment pages. Moms with kids in school can keep together information about school activities and equipment or items needed for extracurricular activities.
- *Prayer Journal*: A great place to write prayer needs for individual family members and friends. It can also serve as a journal to write out prayers and keep Bible verses that mean something special.
- *Sermon/Speaker Notes*: If you enjoy taking notes on seminar speakers or sermons, this is a perfect place to do so.
- *Borrow/Lend Record*: I lend a lot of resources to others, so this helps me keep track of who has which book or tape of mine. When I go to look for that item and can't find it on the bookshelf, I know who has it. Borrowed items can also be noted to remind you of the need to return them and to whom. During one pregnancy, several women loaned me maternity clothes. I used my notebook to briefly describe each item and who it belonged to. This helped greatly when returning the clothes several months later.
- *Telephone and Address*: If you don't have a telephone and address book, starting one in a planner is a good idea.
- *Plastic Zip Pouch*: A plastic pouch can hold paper clips, a highlighter, sticky notes, and other odds and ends. You might want to add other pouches, such as one for keeping sales receipts.
- *Correspondence Diary*: This section helps to keep track of cards sent, notes written, and thank you notes mailed out. This is also a good place to jot down names of people who need a thank you

note in appreciation for something they gave you or did for you. Before I kept a correspondence diary, I had difficulty remembering if I just intended to send someone a card or if I had really done so. Keeping track of my written communication assured me of what I had or hadn't done.

Each mother will have her own ideas for the sections she could use in a notebook or planner. Our needs are so individual that we need to be creative and flexible to make it work for us.

TIME AND INFORMATION MANAGEMENT

The profession of motherhood does not operate as many professions do with a tight schedule of appointments, meetings, and deadlines. Instead, we have a lot of information we are responsible to organize and a lot of people we need to assist. As the children grow older, the meetings, sports schedules, and appointments increase. If a method of organization is in place, it will help you manage your responsibilities as the activities multiply.

Just like other professions, motherhood requires the use of good time and resource management. As we dedicate our bright minds and exceptional skills to the profession of motherhood, we must not forget time and information management. I can't get much done without my planner—and, of course, a good supply of sticky notes!

———— A STEP FURTHER. . . ————

List the areas of your life that need organization. Make a check mark next to those areas that could become a part of your planner.

෧ඁ

Based upon the information you want to organize, what type and size of planner would work best for you?

Investigate the different planner options available (electronic, preprinted, and self-created). Compare size, cost, and practicality.

∽

Ask three friends what tool they use to organize their time and information. Brainstorm with them your planner needs. We can learn so much from other women in the profession of motherhood!

part 4

ESTABLISH YOUR CAREER TRAINING AND DEVELOPMENT

chapter 13

DEVELOP YOUR PARTNERSHIP WITH GOD

I WENT TO SCHOOL FOR FOUR YEARS TO GET MY BACHELOR OF MUSIC Education degree. Although I planned on using my education to teach, our children entered into the picture earlier than we had anticipated. Now I'm spending more than twenty years of my life doing a job for which I have absolutely no education or training. There are many days I ask myself, "What am I doing?"

Most of us in the profession of motherhood ask ourselves this at one time or another. *The key, though, is not to get stuck in the feeling of helplessness, but to seek out the education we need to be the parents God called us to be.*

I used to say that there was no guidebook or training course for marriage or parenting, but I found that I was wrong. There is a guide-book for raising children and having a strong marriage: it's called the Bible. God has much to say about the responsibility of raising chil-dren. I have found the Bible to be my training manual for the profes-sion of motherhood. It is a manual rich in information, principles, and guidelines for life.

As we look at the Bible, we need to have an understanding of the concept of absolute truth. With that understanding, we can begin to look at some of the specific ways we can develop a partnership with God as we seek career training and development as mothers.

ABSOLUTE TRUTH VS. MORAL RELATIVISM

We live in a very high-tech society. Our forms of entertainment (reading, television, movies) and our methods of communication (email, Internet) have great impact on our lives. They influence our thinking, our expectations, and our value system. The messages come fast and furious. They tell us how we should look, how we should feel, how we should dress, how we should parent, how we should keep our homes, and even how we should approach our marriages. Unfortunately though, it is often not good, correct, or even truthful information. The messages convey a very self-seeking, child-centered, and godless point of view. If we buy into the messages our culture sends us, we are headed for a life of confusion and frustration because we really aren't operating the way God designed for us to live life.

Think of it this way, have you ever purchased a new appliance for your home? After you install it you have two choices: to operate it without reading the instructions, or to read the instructions and then use the appliance as it was designed to be used.

If we decide not to read the instructions (which many of us do!) we may never fully understand the value of this piece of equipment and we may miss out on some of the unique features it offers us. We might only use half of its capabilities. Perhaps we'd use it inappropriately, in a way that it was not designed to be used, and even damage it.

Instead, we could read the instructions and possibly be surprised by what we learn. We may not have fully understood its value and unique design when we purchased it, but now we find out all of the tricks it can perform and discover all of its capabilities. At the same time we learn about its boundaries, limitations, and warnings. Now we have learned not only the "dos" but also the "don'ts" of using it.

The instruction manual for a home appliance is written by the one(s) who designed and created the appliance. The designers know both its capabilities and its limitations. They understand its value and want to communicate that information to you, the owner.

Do you see the parallel with God's Word, the Bible? God, our creator and designer, has written an instruction manual for life, filled with incredible insight into both our capabilities and our limitations. In communicating to us our value and our design, He also presented the guidelines for living life, having a successful marriage, and being a good parent. If we read the book and follow the instructions, we'll be better equipped.

The Bible is truth. Absolute truth. It is timeless. It doesn't change based upon our moods, our circumstances, or our feelings. There is right and there is wrong. *Absolute truth exists to protect us from hurt we don't have to experience.*

Our culture, though, bombards us with lies. We live in a society inundated with moral relativism, which says, "I'll decide what is right for me and you decide what is right for you." With moral relativism there is no right or wrong except how you choose to define it for yourself.

With moral relativism, man makes the rules and changes them. With absolute truth, God made the rules and they remain constant.

SPENDING TIME TOGETHER

If you talk with others who have a partnership with Christ, you might hear them talking about having a "quiet time" with God. There's nothing magical about the phrase "quiet time" except that it describes a time we set aside to grow our friendship with God. The best quiet times are when we read the guidebook for life (our Bible) and spend time talking and listening to God in prayer.

Mothers with young children at home have very little, if any, quiet time. The concept is foreign to most of us. Even if I get up before my children to find some quiet moments in the morning, I find they only get up earlier, too. If I look for quiet time in the evening before I go to bed, I find I'm too tired. We have people pulling at us from all sides at all hours of the day. If we are creative, though, we can carve out time throughout our day to develop our friendship with God. So how can we rise to the challenge?

I once heard Donna Otto speak about the subject of spending time with God. She shared the idea of having a "prayer basket" in which you keep your Bible, a notebook for prayer requests and journaling, note cards to send to friends you have prayed for, and several pens. This prayer basket holds all of the items needed for a quiet time. One simple grasp of the handle allows you to capitalize on the moments you find to read and pray.

As professional mothers we have to learn to operate within the seasons of motherhood when it comes to growing our friendship with God. The preschool season of motherhood demands hands-on child rearing almost all day. If you have a baby and a toddler, you are not even assured of having one hour during the day when they are both taking a nap. I remember my friend Janice lamenting in the midst of mothering her three preschoolers, "I feel like all I'm getting is snacks with God, and I want a meal." She was spending time with God, but it was more like sharing cookies and milk rather than a steak dinner.

When I had several small children, I found it worked well to keep a small Bible in each of our bathrooms. Although I wasn't always assured of going to the bathroom alone, it did happen every once in a while, and, if I was lucky I could steal a few extra moments refueling myself with God's promises.

Perhaps your kids are older. You may spend time waiting at piano lessons, or you may have some time to yourself while they play at the park or the beach. Pick up an extra Bible (for about $5 or less) just to keep in your "waiting bag" or in the car for times like these. It will be there waiting for you whenever you have a few moments to spend in the Word of God.

READING THE BIBLE

One summer several years ago, I was approached by a young mom in our neighborhood. She had recently said yes to a friendship with God and wanted to build that relationship. She had two other friends who also wanted to know more. They wondered if I would be willing to meet with them one morning each week throughout the summer.

We began meeting on a Tuesday morning in June and I soon realized all three of these women were truly beginning a relationship with

Christ. None had grown up in the church, and not one of them had any basic Bible knowledge. We were starting at the very beginning.

Examining our desire is the first step in successfully reading the Bible. It doesn't matter where we start—what matters is the condition of our hearts. Do we want to learn? Do we desire to look for truth to guide our lives? Do we want to really know God?

Second, we need to have a version of the Bible that we can read with ease. Many versions of the Bible are available to us. The words "thee" and "thou" aren't commonly used anymore, so trying to wade through that type of vocabulary in the King James Version will only complicate our study. Look for a Bible that uses today's language. The NIV (New International Version) or the NKJV (New King James Version) are good choices.

Third, consider getting a study Bible. The additional notes will further explain the text. It's almost like having a teacher right there with you each time you read. Study Bibles also explain details about each book of the Bible—why it was written, who wrote it, the topics covered, why it is important, and so on. This can prove very helpful in a growing relationship with God.

Developing a friendship with God happens when we learn more about God, His design for us, and His guidelines for life. Reading the Bible and talking with God are two very important keys to a successful partnership with God. As we grow closer to God, we will also learn to recognize when He is speaking to us.

HOW DOES GOD SPEAK TO US?

A one-way friendship isn't much of a friendship at all. When only one person in the relationship does all the talking, it hampers the friendship. Our friendship with God is no different. God does speak to us, but it usually is not in an audible voice like we would speak to one another. If we don't understand the different ways God speaks, we will miss that part of the relationship.

God often speaks to us through His Word, the Bible. Do you remember when I shared in chapter 5 about the difficulties in my marriage and how God convicted me when I read in the Bible about removing the plank in my own eye before removing the splinter from my husband's eye? Without a doubt, God spoke to me that day through His Word. It was clear. My heart and His heart connected.

Sometimes God speaks to us through people. Recently I had a friend share with me a story of how God had provided for her family in a very special way. As she spoke about the way He worked, I knew without a doubt God was speaking to me through her saying, "Jill, I can be trusted. I will take care of you, too. Do not worry." God also uses people around us to speak His truth just when we need it. In a world of relativism, God's truth is a message we need to hear.

A third way that God speaks to people is through the direct leading of the Holy Spirit. Some people describe this as the nudges God gives. During the writing of this book, I had a friend who was awakened in the middle of the night and was prompted to pray for me. She didn't know why she needed to pray, but she couldn't ignore the nudge to pray. Little did she know that I had also awakened in the night and couldn't sleep. Getting out of bed at 2 A.M., I had decided to work on one of the book chapters. I needed prayer at just that time. When God speaks to us through promptings, sometimes they don't make sense. We have to trust, though, that God is all-knowing, while we have limited knowledge. He just asks us to trust His lead.

How can we know that it is God speaking to us? First, we must remember that God will never contradict Himself. We know about God through the Bible. We can compare what we're hearing with what the Bible says about God. Several years ago I was mentoring a young woman in her marriage. They had a difficult relationship at best. Both husband and wife needed to face the destruction they were bringing to their marriage. One morning she showed up at my house and stated that God had spoken to her. He told her to divorce her husband. We talked further and I shared with her that God couldn't possibly have told her that because that would be contradictory to His Word. God's plan for marriage to be a lifetime commitment and His strong words against divorce are clearly communicated in the Bible. God will never contradict Himself. As He speaks to us, it will always be in accordance with His Word and who He is.

WHAT AM I FEEDING MY MIND?

When I was in college, I was required to take a computer class. The class was primarily based on programming for mainframe computers. (Obviously, this was before the personal computer revolution!) My mind is not designed for computer programming at all. I remember doing everything I could to just get by in that class. But there is one concept I learned from that course that has stuck with me: GIGO—Garbage In, Garbage Out.

Basically this means that computers can only process what is entered into them. If you put garbage in, you get garbage out. You can take that same concept and apply it to your life. If you put garbage into your mind, you find your actions are a reflection of that garbage. You need to ask yourself, "What am I feeding my mind?"

As we look to develop ourselves as professional mothers we need to evaluate what messages we are taking in (and exposing our children to)—what are we reading, what are we watching, what are we listening to, and who are we spending time with? These greatly affect the kind of wives and mothers we are. Let's look at each for a moment:

Reading

Novels—If you are a novel reader, are you reading novels that encourage marriage or glamorize relationships outside of marriage? If your idea of a good novel is the latest by Danielle Steele you might instead try books written by Jeannette Oke or Terry Blackstock. These romance novels are written with Christian morals woven into the story.

Magazines—If you enjoy reading magazines, be careful what you subscribe to. If your choices are *Mademoiselle* or *Redbook,* consider replacing them with *Today's Christian Woman, Marriage Partnership,* or *Focus on the Family* magazines. These magazines present relevant articles about topics that impact your life. They do so within the boundaries of God's truth.

Books—We live in a time that has seen the most self-help books ever published. There is much to choose from when it comes to finances, parenting, marriage, career, personality, and more. Be careful of what you are reading when you are looking to expand your knowledge. If you aren't accustomed to shopping in a Christian bookstore for self-help books, consider expanding your horizons.

Listening and Watching

Radio—What are you listening to on the radio? Are you filling your mind with messages of forbidden romance and broken marriages? Did you know that Christian radio exists? Its rhythm and beat are similar to secular radio stations, yet the messages are encouraging and speak God's truth. Try *Family Radio* for inspirational and uplifting broadcasts of music, news, features on marriage and parenting, and Bible reading. (Go to *familyradio.com* to locate a station near you.)

TV—Be careful of the time spent in front of the TV. Soap operas will do nothing but cause you to be dissatisfied with your marriage and expose you to the idea that adultery is a perfectly natural, even acceptable, part of life. Many sitcoms reek of anti-family, anti-marriage messages. Even the commercials can have a powerful impact on our minds if we are not discerning. When our kids are old enough to understand what's being said on radio and TV, our choices then influence them as well.

Movies—Movies are considered one of the top entertainment options. There are some wonderful movies available that touch either our hearts or our funny bones (sometimes both!). But unfortunately there are far more movies that present moral relativism as perfectly acceptable. These shows erode our sense of right and wrong based upon the absolute truth God has set forth. Before you watch a TV show or a movie, it's important to ask yourself, "How is this going to affect my role as a wife and mother and my friendship with God? Will this be honoring to God?"

Spending Free Time

Friends—We may tell our children, "You are who you hang out with." It is a true statement. Our friendships do have an impact on us. If you are spending time with friends who live according to moral relativism, you will find yourself influenced by their lack of values. Although we need to spend time with a variety of people, those you spend the most time with need to be carefully selected for being encouragers—not discouragers—of your faith and values.

I AM A NEW CREATION

Your life is like a garden. The soil must be worked. Weeding needs to take place. Fertilizer needs to be applied. Water has to be supplied. The results of this work can be seen in beautiful growth in your heart. It's all orchestrated by the Master Gardener who is in the business of growing beautiful lives.

Life with God is a continual process of growth. When we say yes to God, He begins a work in us that will continue throughout our entire lives. He nurtures us like a gardener nurtures his growing plants. As we grow to know God more, He matures us to provide the attitude, the atmosphere, the reflection of Christ that our family so strongly needs.

Life with God is a journey—a journey of growth, encouragement, hope, and joy. Even in the midst of difficulties or sadness, life with God provides us the strength and encouragement to keep going.

As we look for personal growth opportunities in the profession of motherhood, we will find that God has an array of character-growing lessons for us to learn. He wants to grow our integrity. He wants us to value and protect relationships. He wants us to find our value in Him. As we do so, we will be able to move beyond the cries of a world that marches to the beat of a different drum.

God wants us to live life according to His design. He created us and He has given us many guidelines for finding the fulfillment in life that we so much desire. He desires to have a friendship with us. As we grow that friendship, we truly can become the wives and mothers we want to be.

If our job is about influencing the world by raising Godly children, we must be about growing ourselves first. We don't have to have all the answers—we just need to know where to find them. As we spend time with God in prayer, as we read His Word, and as we carefully select what we feed our minds, we will find we are laying the foundation for our value system. Realize today that the single most important career training you can do for your profession as a mother is to nurture and deepen your partnership with God.

―――――――――― **A STEP FURTHER. . .** ――――――――――

What was your home internship experience with the Bible? If a new internship is in order, set three goals for yourself to learn more about God's guidebook for life, the Bible.

൭ൟ

In what areas of your life have you bought the world's messages of moral relativism?

൭ൟ

As you evaluate what you are feeding your mind, list three specific areas where you can make better choices.

chapter 14

PARENT WITH PURPOSE

MOTHERHOOD IS ONE OF THE FEW CAREERS IN WHICH THE GOAL IS TO actually work yourself out of a job. Every day we move one step closer to the ultimate goal of raising children who will be competent, confident, and caring adults. If indeed we are preparing our children for adult life, we need to be purposeful about teaching and training. In fact, that is our primary responsibility—to teach and train. The world we live in is a crazy place. It takes wisdom to learn to navigate the waters of life. Those who are well equipped best handle the twists and turns of real life.

Our task as parents is to equip our children for life on their own. We accomplish this by being available to our children, guiding them as they make their journey of childhood. Additionally we must monitor their media and help them learn relationship skills, discernment, and obedience. Ultimately, we want them to develop their own friendship with God that will equip them for a lifetime.

In parenting we are teaching all the time, but sometimes we are unaware of the lessons our children are learning from us. Our lives serve as a behavioral example for our growing children. As we explore the concept of parenting on purpose, it is important to understand just how much our children are watching us.

MORE IS CAUGHT THAN TAUGHT

Several years ago, we determined that, for a season of time, the best schooling option for two of our children was home schooling. Anne, then in seventh grade, was home for one year. We chose to home school Evan in fifth and sixth grades. During that unique season of motherhood, I learned just how much our children learn from witnessing our every day actions. One particular lesson made a powerful impact on me.

It was a Tuesday afternoon in March, and Anne and Evan were doing some independent work in their bedrooms. Mark and I had a disagreement that led to some conflict before he left for work that morning. I had replayed our discussion in my mind several times, prayed about it, and determined that I had been inappropriate in my communication during our interaction. I knew I needed to make amends for my part in the conflict. Because I had a quiet moment, I decided to call Mark at work to apologize and ask for forgiveness. When I dialed I only got his answering machine, so I left a message offering my apology and desire for forgiveness. Mark came home that evening and offered his forgiveness and apologized for his own role in the conflict. We resolved it and moved on.

The next afternoon Anne, Evan, and I were driving to piano lessons. It was quiet in the car for a few miles until Anne broke the silence. She said, "Mom, you know it was really a cool thing when you called Dad yesterday and apologized to him and asked for his forgiveness." I was stunned. First, I couldn't believe that she had actually heard me make the phone call—she was supposed to be in her bedroom! And second, I was amazed at the influence it had on her. I could have told her over and over about the value of a heartfelt apology and the importance of forgiveness. I could have lectured her on the ins and outs of conflict resolution. But those were not necessary. I taught her more by modeling the appropriate actions.

With children, more is caught than taught. They will learn (good or bad!) by watching us. We can tell them over and over the value of a principle, but by seeing it in action, they will grasp the reality of it. It's not that we shouldn't teach values verbally—we should. But be careful not to exhibit "do as I say, not as I do" behavior. This only confuses children. As far as being godly examples for our children, we need to not only "talk the talk" but "walk the walk" as well.

PROACTIVE VS. REACTIVE PARENTING

Let's consider the difference between proactive and reactive parenting. When it comes to teaching children we often think of the words "discipline," "punishment," or "consequences," which seem such negative terms. If we find ourselves teaching primarily in times of conflict, then we are parenting reactively. This is the most ineffective way to parent.

Our goal needs to be to parent proactively. We need to be a step ahead of our children. We need to know their strengths and their weaknesses, and we need to lead them accordingly. We need to teach, not bark orders. We need to lead, not pull along. We need to train, not expect perfection.

When Austin was three, we wanted him to learn first time obedience, meaning we wanted him to respond to our instructions the first time he heard them, not after we had counted to three or given him multiple warnings. If you've ever tried to get a child dressed in the morning and have chased him or her all over the house, only succeeding in putting on one piece of clothing every five minutes, you will understand the value of first time obedience. If I say, "Austin, please come here," I need a response of "Yes, Mommy," followed by the appropriate action. If Austin is walking down the sidewalk toward the road, I want to be able to say, "Austin, stop!" and have him obey. And ultimately one day I want him to hear God's voice and to be obedient.

I found myself sitting in a doctor's office one afternoon with all four children. The doctor was running late, and we had been warned of the wait ahead of us. I decided to use this time wisely to begin teaching Austin first-time obedience and the verbal response. I told the three older children of my idea for the use of our time. My captive audience thought it might be fun, so we began having each of the older children model the appropriate behavior. I would say, "Anne, please come here," and she would respond with "Yes, Mom" and come sit on my knee (picture this in your mind—Anne was fourteen at the time!). We then continued with Evan and Erica playing the game. Before long Austin wanted to do it, too. He was beginning to catch on to the appropriate response to the request.

Forty-five minutes later, the doctor arrived and we were all weary of our little game, but important groundwork had been laid. Mark and I now had a foundation to which Austin had been exposed. We spent the next few weeks reinforcing this teaching through further training and practice, and eventually we initiated appropriate consequences if Austin did not respond the first time called. Over time the need for consequences dwindled as he soon understood what was expected of him.

Our children need to know what is expected of them. Here are some of the basics they need to be taught:

- the standard for appropriate behavior
- the importance of respecting authority
- how to operate within boundaries
- the need to accept consequences

If they do not understand these concepts, they will have a rude awakening some day when they hold a job in the real world.

Have you ever taken your child to the store only to have him ask for one thing after another? Ask yourself: Have I ever told my child what I expected from him before we entered the store (proactive parenting), or do I find myself battling him throughout the entire shopping trip (reactive parenting)? Children will often rise to the standards if they know them. If they do choose to misbehave, we have the assurance that they knew what was expected of them, freeing us to issue consequences without hesitation or second thoughts. All too often parents punish a child who never knew what was expected of him in the first place.

As our children grow older we must adapt our teaching methods. For example, Mark and I wanted to make sure that our older children knew how to handle introductions and extend hospitality. After all, they don't learn the social graces by osmosis—we have to teach them! Capitalizing on times when we were getting ready for an event where they might be meeting new people (wedding, graduation, new church, etc.), we prepared them for what situations may arise and how they should handle them. Following an evening meal, we would take some time to discuss proper introduction etiquette. With role playing and some practice they soon became more comfortable with a firm hand-shake and a clear "It's nice to meet you."

What are the benefits of proactive parenting? Our children will learn to trust our lead, know they can depend on us, and find security in their family. Our goal is to encourage them to choose to be followers of their parents and a leader of their peers. We, as parents, need to equip them to do both.

MONITOR THEIR MEDIA

Our children are heavily influenced by the world around them. This generation of children has had more media exposure than any previous generation. Television, movies, video games, magazines, books, and music have a profound and lasting impact upon their young minds. One of the benefits of choosing motherhood as your career is that you can determine a strategy and devote your time to monitor your child's interaction with media.

On one hand, the media can be wonderful tools to expand our knowledge. On the other hand, they can be filled with pitfalls. See your role as providing direction for your children. Remember GIGO? This concept takes full effect in the lives of our children, too. It's Garbage In, Garbage Out. Because they are in the formative years of their lives, we need to be especially careful about what goes in their minds.

Let's take a look at some of the media available to children and some positive direction we can provide.

TELEVISION

What is happening in a child's mind hour after hour in front of the TV? Quite a lot! Their minds are formulating right and wrong. They are learning about how people handle conflict (most of the time inappropriately). From the afternoon sitcoms they are discovering that parents are bumbling idiots who really don't have a clue. The evening police shows provide them with large doses of sexuality and are more soap opera than action or adventure. Your teens are being exposed to nighttime teen soap operas that often reek with moral relativism and sexual promiscuity. Do you consider watching cartoons a harmless activity? Look again and watch with a discerning eye. Too many of these "made for children" shows carry adult themes, filled with violence and sexual innuendoes. Are the shows your children are watching complementing your teaching or discrediting it? Beware of what they might be exposed to at a friend's home as well.

The key to using television as an asset is to monitor its use. Consider requiring permission to turn it on, rather than allowing it to be used at any time. Carefully choose which shows they can watch ahead of time. If at all possible, watch television with your children to discuss what is watched. If your child visits a friend's home for a play date, let the parent in charge know what your "policy" is on media they might be exposed to.

Anne and I were watching a Hallmark "Hall of Fame" movie one night. It was what my husband might call a "chick flick." When the show paused for a commercial break, we were exposed to a commercial that was very sexual in nature. It showed a man and a woman who had just met and were very attracted to one another. The commercial insinuated that a sexual tryst was to follow. All this during the commercial break!

I decided to use this as a teaching time for Anne. Our conversation went something like this:

> Me: What were they selling on that commercial, Anne?
>
> Anne: Oatmeal, mom.
>
> Me: I know that, but what else were they selling?
>
> Anne: I don't know.
>
> Me: That commercial was using sex to sell their product, so in a way they were giving a strong, but incorrect message about sex.
>
> Anne: Oh.
>
> Me: Was the sex they were suggesting going to be shared by a husband and a wife?

Anne: No, they had just met each other.

Me: Do you see how this commercial presented the idea that sex outside of marriage is perfectly okay?

Anne: Yes, I didn't even think about that.

Me: Sex is a beautiful gift that God has given to married couples, but the world has distorted its purposes. Many times the things we read or watch may have hidden messages that we need to be aware of. That's what we just saw in this commercial. It is important that we learn to discern the communication the world sends us so we don't unintentionally buy into its false messages.

As mothers, if we do not watch with a discerning eye those messages can influence us, too. We need to be discerning for our children's sake, and we need to teach them to be discerning themselves.

MAGAZINES

Dozens of books and magazines are marketed to teenagers. Girls especially are influenced by magazines like *Seventeen*, *YM*, and others. The messages within many of those pages are not supportive of the teaching you do as a parent. In fact, they often oppose your values. What else is out there? Focus on the Family (1–800–A FAMILY) has a wonderful line of magazines for children and teenagers. Their *Brio* magazine for teen girls offers articles on fashion, music, hair and makeup, and boys. For teen boys, *Breakaway* magazine gives the latest information about music, school issues, and relationships. Both publications are trendy, relevant magazines that are Christ centered. They will encourage your values rather than contradict them, and they will encourage your child's faith.

BOOKS

Many girls enjoy reading romance novels, but the sexuality presented on the pages of popular authors such as Danielle Steel and the Harlequin Romance novels is detrimental to a teen who is learning right and wrong. Instead of these, help your daughter to consider all the other well-written novels and the classics, as well as faith-building nonfiction books. If your daughter must read romance, encourage her to read romance novels written by Christian authors Jeannette Oke, Terry Blackstock, Jane Peart, or Lori Wicke. These books can often be found in a public library under "Inspirational Reading" or purchased at a Christian bookstore. Of course, one of the numerous teen study or devotional Bibles on the market may capture their interest as well. Many of these have devotions that deal with how to handle peer pressure, dating, and other teen issues.

MUSIC

The messages found in music can have a profound effect as they erode the moral fabric of a child's heart. Focus on the Family's magazine and website, *Plugged In,* is a wonderful resource for parents who want to know more about the music teens listen to. Call 1–800–A FAMILY or try their website at *www.family.org.* Christian contemporary is a rapidly expanding music market. If we give children a taste for this music early on (many songs have scriptural messages), they may continue to choose to listen to it as they grow older. One of the best labels for Christian contemporary is Integrity Music (go to *www.integritymusic.com*). Check out your local Christian bookstore when searching for positive music alternatives.

MOVIES

Today's youth have been exposed to more scenes of sex and violence than any other generation because of the film industry. Often movies that are rated PG or PG–13 contain scenes that can compromise the innocence of a child. Parents need to know where they can find relevant information concerning the content of movies available at the theater or the local video store. Several websites have been developed to assist parents in monitoring their child's movie viewing. As a parent, I have found these very helpful.

www.family.org/pluggedin
www.gospelcom.net/preview/
www.screenit.com

INTERNET

The Internet is a wonderful technology and media resource, but it needs to be used with parent guidance. Don't be naïve about your child's ability to maneuver through the internet and end up in places he or she shouldn't be. It can easily happen by accident and far too often it happens purposefully. Children are naturally inquisitive. They will explore and see what they can find. If you have Internet access in your home, make sure a filter is in place to help protect the innocence of your children and teens. Internet services such as AOL and MSN have parent controls that should be put in place. Our family has chosen to use a complete filtered Internet service called Cleanweb (*www.cleanweb.net*). Software is also available (*www.cybersitter.com*) to provide additional protection against access to objectionable material on the Internet.

LEARN TO DISCERN

The answer to the media's heavy influence on our children lies far beyond trying to simply shield our children from these messages. One of the most important tools we can give our children is a discerning heart and eye. Discernment is defined as "having or showing good judgment or understanding." When our children understand the value of discernment and are equipped with the necessary tools, they are on their way to being prepared for adulthood.

In order to be discerning, the first thing needed is an understanding of absolute truth and moral relativism. Children must understand what is right and why it is right, and what is wrong and why it is wrong. Next, they need the awareness that the world around them communicates messages that they will need to evaluate and be prepared to turn away from.

I remember struggling with this as a teenager myself as I weighed the very different messages between the world and what I heard at church and home. I didn't understand what to do with the two contrasting messages and felt unprepared for the pressure I faced. I found myself living a double life—I acted one way at school and with friends, another way at home and church. It was a terrible predicament to be in and the choices I made were less than ideal.

We need to prepare our children for the various messages they will hear. We need to equip them with the tools to know how to live in the world but not be of it. We need to teach them to be discerning through knowing God's Word.

We've had to explain to our children why they could not watch certain TV shows that some of their friends are allowed to view. Asking them to identify some of the hidden messages they've seen on commercials for these shows has been very helpful in helping them discern the appropriateness of the show.

More recently, we've been helping our older children navigate appropriate boy/girl relationships. We've talked about the abstinence message and how misleading the goal of abstinence really is. We've introduced them to the concept of purity, which means not even walking down the road of sexual temptation. When others are playing the dating game, we've challenged them to operate differently from many of their classmates. When children are equipped with alternate options instead of the world's way of doing things, they are more able to make good choices.

RELATIONSHIP MANAGEMENT

We all experience times when we do not see eye to eye with those closest to us. God has created all of us with unique ways of processing information, special talents and giftedness, and personal opinions about life. It is inevitable that at times we will conflict with those around us. Because we are unique, our ideas, opinions, and emotions may at times clash with those closest to us.

Many of us reach adulthood and still don't have a good foundation and understanding of healthy relational skills. We may have been raised in a home in which conflict was handled with rage. Maybe conflict seemed not to exist in your home, always being swept under the carpet. It's possible that you became a peacemaker who avoids conflict and tries to make everyone happy. Some of us have been taught to talk to everyone else about a problem except the person we have the problem with. In reality, this is gossip, and it is detrimental to relationships.

God teaches us how to handle conflict. In Matthew 18:15, He says, "If your brother sins against you, go and show him his fault, just between the two of you." We need to go to the person who hurt us to mend the relationship before we talk to anyone else about the problem. When we promptly follow God's guidelines, we can resolve conflict before bitterness sets in. We need to operate that way as adults and we need to teach our children the same.

One of your goals as a mother is to help your children recognize conflict and equip them with the tools to bring about resolution. What are those tools?

- cooperation
- sharing
- active listening
- offering an apology and asking for forgiveness
- accepting an apology and extending forgiveness

Let's take a moment to consider the value of a full apology, because even as adults we sometimes offer only half apologies. This is why we often feel our conflicts are never fully resolved. We stop after "I'm sorry" and leave it there. But there is another part of an apology that is very important. It is a request for forgiveness. "I'm sorry for [identify the offense]. I realize by doing that I caused you [identify the hurt]. Will you please forgive me?" is the full expression of apology. The one who was hurt or offended should then bring full closure to the hurt by eventually responding with forgiveness (verbally expressing, "I forgive you").

Our children need to understand the importance of mending relationships. They need to respect and value both family members and friends. They need good relationship management skills. We start by learning these skills ourselves and then we teach them to our children.

VALUING GOD'S WORD

We've already discussed the need to know where to find absolute truth. Our children have the same need. When faced with a decision, they need to know where they will find the answer. They need to value and understand God's Word as the one source that will give them the answers to life's questions and problems.

When Anne and Evan were small, I used to get frustrated when they awoke shortly after I did in the morning, only to interrupt my few quiet moments to read the Bible. But I soon realized the value of this interaction. They found me reading my Bible. Once again, it was the power of influence at work. I could tell them of the importance of the Bible and God's truth, but until they saw me use it to guide my life, my words were hollow. After God changed my perspective, I thanked Him for every time I was interrupted from that point on.

When our children were toddlers, we gave each of them a small, inexpensive Bible. We found some stickers with the picture of Jesus on them and pasted them throughout the Bible. The game was to find the picture of Jesus and learn to say his name. As they grew older we bought them a children's Bible that put the Bible in story form, allowing them to learn some key stories of the Bible at their level.

As they grew in their reading skills, we gave them their own complete Bible in a NIV (New International Version) or a NKJV (New King James Version). These versions use more of today's language and are easier to read. They could then carry them to church and use them at home. As they progressed into their teens, they moved on to an NIV Study Bible or the Teen Extreme Bible, which helped them apply God's Word to their lives.

Avoid the temptation to believe that by taking your children to church you are doing your spiritual duty. We have much more work to do than that. We need to encourage them to make a relationship with Jesus a part of their daily lives. Can you think of a higher calling than the career you have chosen?

A FRIENDSHIP WITH GOD

As our children grow into adulthood, our goal is to transfer the yielding of their hearts from our authority and direction to God's. To accomplish that we must be modeling and introducing our children to a friendship with God.

When our children are infants, we can pray over them. This is their initial exposure to talking with God. As they grow older we can help them learn to pray on their own. Here is a great tool to use! When we were teaching each of our children to pray as toddlers we would do a "fill in the blank" prayer. We used the ACTS acronym to expand the way they talked with God each evening before bed. A is Adoration, C-Confession, T-Thanksgiving, and S-Supplication. Mark or I would say the sentence and then we would let the child fill in the blank. It went something like this:

> *God,*
> *I praise you because you are* _____ *[big, loving, caring].*
> *I'm sorry that I* _____. *Thank you for forgiving me.*
> *Thank you for* _____.
> *Please help* _____.
> *I love you, Jesus. Amen.*

Over time, we would say less and less, and they would pick up more of the prayer. Sometimes we would help jog their memories about things they needed to apologize for or things to be thankful for. But it was the process of leading them that was important. By the time they hit grade school, they had a sense of communication with God. They understood why and how we talk with Him. They were equipped to continue their journey to know God.

When should we pray with our children? Any time prayer is needed. But that is easier said than done for most of us. Many of us didn't have prayer modeled for us outside of meals and bedtime. But if those are the only times we encourage our children to pray, we are limiting their communication with God.

The Savage family has continued to grow in prayer over the years. When Erica was in second grade, she attended a Christian school. Whenever her class would hear a police or ambulance siren throughout the day, the teacher encouraged them to pause and pray for the person who might be hurt. Erica brought this home to our family as well. If we are driving through town and hear a siren, Erica will say "Mom, we have to pray." I usually tell her to go right ahead and pray—I pray along (with my eyes open, of course!) as she prays aloud.

This is one little exercise that has helped us move prayer beyond meals and bedtime.

Two years ago we moved to a different level of prayer. Anne was going back to public school after a year of home schooling, and I wanted to send her well equipped for anything she might face. The one-hour school bus ride posed more problems than the six-hour school day, and I especially wanted her to be able to handle the pressure on the bus. My friend Holly introduced me to the concept of "kitchen door prayers" that she had developed with her eight children over the years. She suggested that I walk with Anne to the door as she prepared to leave. Pausing at the door, I prayed aloud for Anne asking for wisdom, discernment, and courage. I also prayed for anything specific that I knew would be in her day (tests, field trips, etc.). At first this was a little uncomfortable for both of us, but we quickly moved beyond any uneasiness as it soon became a necessary part of our morning. If we missed it for any reason, we both felt the void.

About three months into the school year, Anne said she wanted to pray for her friends during those kitchen door prayers. We decided we would begin "kitchen island" prayers as we moved to yet another level of praying together. We began to pray for Anne's day and the challenges ahead about five minutes before the bus was to arrive, and she began praying for her friends and other things I hadn't been aware of. It proved to be not only beneficial spiritually but also relationally for us. Through prayer I was beginning to know more about her world.

A year later when Evan went back to public school after two years of home schooling, we went one step further with our morning prayer time. All six of us now gather fifteen minutes before leaving for school to pray for each other and the people who our lives will intersect with that day. We have found the time spent together in prayer is precious. Is it difficult to get everyone ready fifteen minutes early? I would have to answer yes. Is it worth it? Absolutely!

OUR HIGH CALLING AS MOTHERS

The profession of motherhood is an ever-changing adventure. Just when you think you've got it under control, your child enters a new developmental stage! As our children continue to change we need to learn more about parenting and about our children as individuals.

Recently, I've been struck with how often I parent my children as a group, rather than as unique individuals. I've asked God to help me see them as the uniquely created people they are. I want them to feel like individuals rather than a group project. God is expanding my vision once again.

Parenting proactively needs to be a primary goal for those of us in the profession of motherhood. Not only will we find the parenting process more enjoyable, we'll also find it a more effective method of teaching children. Equipping our children with the tools of absolute truth will help them to live in a world of moral relativism. Introducing our children to a friendship with God will give them a friend like no other. We are raising the next generation and this is the focus of our profession.

As we consider the essential elements of our career training and development, let us not miss out on our high calling as mothers and the need to educate ourselves when it comes to parenting. Parent with purpose—it's one of the most important responsibilities we have in the profession of motherhood.

───────── A STEP FURTHER. . . ─────────

Think about the "more caught than taught" theory and identify two times you taught your children something (good or bad) by your behavior.

೧൦

Identify two times that you parented proactively.

೧൦

Identify two times that you parented reactively. If you could go back in time, how would you have handled those situations differently?

What adjustments do you need to make when you evaluate what your children are exposed to in the following types of media? Use the GIGO concept to help you discern appropriateness.

Movies
Television
Radio/Music
Magazines
Books
Internet

chapter 15

MAKE YOUR HOUSE A HOME

WHEN OUR MOMS' GROUP BEGAN, WE DISCUSSED HOW WE WOULD USE our time together. We all agreed that learning more about both marriage and parenting was a priority. We wanted to have fun together, too. We looked forward to encouraging one another. But there was an often overwhelming desire to learn how to handle the housekeeping part of being at home—you know, the practical stuff!

The skills of homemaking do not always come naturally in this instant gratification world that we live in. Organization, finances, shopping, cooking, and cleaning take both time and energy. They are skills that must be learned, which makes them an important part of every mother's career training and development.

Years ago women learned these skills from their mothers and grandmothers who lived nearby. In our transient society today many of us live away from those who might teach us the skills of housekeeping. Many of us do live near family, but both mothers and grandmothers work full time. Because of their busy schedules, they are not available for the natural mentoring that used to take place. Still others of us have extended family members who are unwilling or incapable of teaching and training a young mom. And unfortunately there are some who have lost their mothers early in life.

If you have a natural mentor, consider yourself blessed. If you do not, you may need to learn the skills of homemaking from others who are in the trenches of motherhood. I learned much from the women in my moms' group, from reading books, and from my own mother, who lives three hours away but makes herself very available.

When it comes to housekeeping, personal taste and personality type certainly come into play. What is important, though, is that we know ourselves, our goals, and our likes and dislikes. Then we can set our plans into motion.

Because housekeeping is a large part of what a professional mother does, we are going to address the varied, and, yes, mundane tasks that we so often do. We're going to look at strategic ways to approach these important tasks. Keeping a home is part of creating a haven for our family. When we take it seriously, our housekeeping shows the family that we love and value them.

ORGANIZATION

Every time I walked into Sue's house, I knew something was special about it. I would describe it as warm, stable, and even restful. I always felt comfortable in this home that rarely had piles on the kitchen counter. When Sue needed to find something she knew right where it was.

I would often return home discouraged as I looked at my piles and my messes. I would search for hours for a misplaced item that I needed. When I tackled cleaning my home, it would take me hours just to do one room because I spent so much time putting things away just to find the furniture and the floor. Housekeeping was overwhelming to me.

One afternoon Sue was at my home. Our children were playing together, and Sue and I were having a much needed cup of tea. We sat at my kitchen table, scooting aside piles of graduation announcements for my husband's upcoming graduation from college. I was embarrassed by the mess and the clutter. In desperation, I asked my friend, "What should I do with these? If this were your job and these invitations were at your house, where would you put them while you were working on them?" Sue quickly responded, "Do you have a basket? I'd work out of a basket so they could quickly be moved from place to place. This way they will also stay organized and in one place. In other words, Jill, I would give them a home."

Now, I know that may seem like an elementary concept to some of you, but it was new information to me. That day was the beginning of a new thought process for me. The messy mom was learning from the organized mom about the concept of items in my possession having a home. I was being introduced to the concept of "a place for everything and everything in its place." It didn't happen overnight; it took me years to change the way I kept our home. It took me even longer to teach the concept to the other members of the family. But now it is a concept that I own fully and find incredibly freeing when it comes to caring for our home.

These days it takes me just an hour or two to clean the whole house (of course, it depends on how many interruptions I have!) rather than two or three days. I'm truly cleaning, not just putting away. I feel relieved by the organization.

Now, I'm still a messy at heart and can quickly default to my old ways when I'm tired or too busy, so I do have to work harder at it than someone who is a naturally organized person. I also have a daughter who received my messy gene, and we're in the process of training her about the value of everything having a home. She has a sign on her door that says, "You are now entering my mother's nightmare." There are days her room lives up to that description!

Keeping things organized is an important part of respecting property. God asks us to care for the things He has provided for us, so as we take care of our provisions, we communicate value to the One who gave them to us.

PAPER, PAPER, AND MORE PAPER!

One of the most overwhelming parts of organization and housekeeping is what to do with all the paper! There are many books and articles written on home organization, and they have wonderful ideas to stay on top of paper and other materials in our possession.

Let me highlight a few suggestions that have made a difference in our home.

Mail

- Set up a file system in the room where you usually open mail.
- Open mail and immediately throw away the opened envelope.
- Toss junk mail immediately.
- File remaining mail in one of three places:
  1. "Bills to Pay"
  2. "Response Needed"
  3. Other family members' individual files
- Set aside one day each week to handle the "Response Needed" file.

Newspapers, Magazines, Newsletters, and Catalogs

- Read, then toss.
- Tear out articles you want to keep and file them according to topic.
- Put a magazine or two in your "waiting bag" (see chapter 9) or in the car.
- Catalogs can steal your valuable time and cause you to covet a lot of things you don't need. Toss these immediately unless you have an urgent need to order something from them.

School Papers

- Set up three files for each child
  1. "To Keep" (for those things you want to eventually put in his or her keepsake box—clean out monthly)
  2. "Current Info." (for current information about field trips, projects, grades, etc.—clean out weekly)
  3. "Annual Info." (teacher phone numbers, school handbook, immunization records, etc.—clean out each summer)
- Each time you handle your child's school papers, decide whether they need to go in the garbage or in one of the above files. Remember this slogan to avoid creating piles of paper on

your kitchen counter or piles of any other stuff around the house: "Don't put it down, put it away." Teach this one to your kids!

TELEPHONE

- Put all directories (school, church, soccer league, etc.) in one three-ring binder that is stored by the phone in the main living area (at our house, that's the kitchen!). Take the directories apart, if necessary, and punch holes to fit them in the three-ring binder. Use index dividers (which you can purchase at your local office supply store) to separate the different directories. Use an alphabetical index with lined filler paper in each section for your miscellaneous phone numbers.
- Use a phone log for phone messages. A phone log keeps messages in one central place and greatly decreases lost or misplaced pieces of paper. A steno pad makes a great phone log or a smaller three-ring binder (5½" x 8½") with pages you create yourself on your computer work very well. We create our own pages and then run them off on a copier. They look something like this:

Date	Time	Call for	Caller	Message

FINANCES

Each family is unique when it comes to handling finances. In some families the husband pays the bills, while in other families the wife handles those responsibilities. It's not so important who manages the money, it's just important that the money is managed! All too often we let money manage us when we should be the ones who manage the money.

Many of us raising families have rarely, if ever, had to go without much. We are accustomed to instant gratification. "Buy now, pay later" is the battle cry of many families today. This is a dangerous direction to take our finances, though, and we need to be aware of the pitfalls of following the world's messages about finances.

Living on one income necessitates the need for good money management. We are given only so much to spend each month. The goal is not to have more month than money! We also need to learn delayed gratification, which means we wait to purchase items until we can afford them.

One of the best ways to live on one income is to operate within a budget, a valuable tool that allows a family to look at their weekly and monthly needs and then allocate a certain amount of money to each expense area. Having these parameters both mandates and facilitates that spending stay within the budget. For example, if my food budget is $100 a week then I need to be responsible to stay within $100 each week. Our family has also found it very helpful to operate on a cash-only basis. This keeps us from overspending or incurring debt. Larry Burkett's book *The Financial Planning Workbook* was a wonderful resource to this one-income family as it provided many worksheets to help us in our financial planning. It's also important to remember that a budget is flexible. It may need to be adjusted to accommodate changing needs, growing children, or an additional family member.

SHOPPING

I do not enjoy going to the grocery store. I find it very time consuming and energy depleting. After spending hours at the store, standing twenty minutes in the checkout line, and then loading your purchases in your car, you are still not finished. You still have to unload it and put it all away once you get home! It makes me tired just thinking about it.

Shopping is necessary, though, in order to take care of our family. Here are some tips to remember:

- Try to limit how often you shop—try once every two weeks or even once a month. When I began shopping once a month it cut our grocery bill substantially. I do run to the store once a week to pick up bread, milk, and eggs, but I go with just $15 in my purse to keep me from impulse shopping.
- Make a master shopping list on your computer. Ask your grocery store for a layout of their store—most have them readily avail-

able. List your items in the order they are found in the store. This helps you maximize your time and decreases the need to round up items you bypassed on your trip through the store.

- Shop with a list and stick to it! If an item is not on the list, don't buy it.
- Eat before you go to the store. If you are not hungry, you'll be less likely to fill the cart with extra but unnecessary goodies.
- Don't get snagged by the "2 for 1" gimmicks. If the item you want is "2 for $5," but you only need or will only use one, then purchase one for $2.50.
- Try shopping without children—maybe in the evening when your husband can watch them or trade sitting with a friend when it's convenient for both of you. You will be less likely to impulse shop without the kids.

MEALS AND SNACKS

When I stop to think about the amount of time I am in the kitchen each day, it is no wonder I dream of the day I could actually consider the kitchen closed, if only for an hour! The food we prepare for our family is part of caring for their physical needs. Preparing food is an act of love for our families.

I do not particularly enjoy cooking, although I do love to bake. I have found some ways to better manage the twenty-one meals and dozens of snacks I need to prepare each week. Maybe these ideas will get your wheels turning:

- Consider a monthly meal plan. Take a blank calendar and plan your meals for the month. Make your shopping list from your meal plan. Don't forget to figure in days for leftovers and ordering pizza on an extra busy day!
- Cook multiple meals at one time. If you make lasagna, don't just make one pan—make two, three, or even four pans! Then freeze the extra pans for meals later in the month.
- Do once-a-month cooking. To learn more about this concept, pick up the book *Once A Month Cooking* by Mimi Wilson and Mary

Beth Lagerborg, or contact the Thirty-Day Gourmet at 1–800–9 MANUAL. You can also contact Hearts at Home to order a tape of this popular conference workshop we offer at our events. I've been doing once-a-month cooking for the past few years and I love it!

- Start a meal co-op. A popular plan is called "Cooking Among Friends." You can order a handbook to get you started by calling 1(616)895–6909.
- Start preparations for dinner at breakfast. Don't wait until 4 P.M. to think about dinner. Consider getting into the habit of preparing parts of your meals early in the day. This allows for defrosting if necessary and assures you of having all necessary ingredients on hand when you are ready to cook.
- Teach your children how to help in the kitchen and how to cook as soon as they're old enough. Let them assist with meal preparation regularly, and as they grow older occasionally allow them to prepare entire meals.

BAKING

- Bake double recipes of quick breads (pumpkin, banana, poppy seed) and then freeze the extra loaves. This allows for twice as many goodies with half the mess!
- Double your cookie dough recipes. Drop dough by spoonfuls or roll into balls and place on a cookie sheet. Place in the freezer until hard. Put these unbaked, frozen cookies in a freezer bag and pull out as needed to bake fresh homemade cookies without the mess of flour and sugar each time!
- Teach your children to bake as they grow. Allow them to learn to measure and mix the ingredients. Don't forget to teach them the importance of cleaning up the mess, too!

HOUSE

The condition of our homes is one of personal preference. Some of us vacuum every day, while others vacuum once a week. Some of us dust weekly, while others aren't bothered by a little dust and choose to dust about twice a month or as needed.

General cleanliness is important for the basic health of our family. Our goal is to keep germs at bay and to provide a relatively comfortable home for our family and the occasional houseguest.

A smart woman once said, "A perfect house is the sign of a wasted life." That is a good statement to remember when you're feeling sad because your house is imperfect. It also keeps housekeeping in perspective: We are in effect wasting time in striving to make the house look perfect.

Our moms' group recently discussed the challenges of keeping house. Here are some of the suggestions we shared:

Cleaning

- A picked-up house will look clean, but a cluttered house will always look dirty. Keep things picked up and you will feel like the house is clean most of the time.
- Consider one or two cleaning jobs each day rather than trying to do it all in one day. This is especially helpful when you have small children and little time.
- If you insist upon cleaning all in one day, turn the phone off, turn up the stereo and stay as focused as a mother with children at home possibly can!
- Give the kids their own dusting cloths and let them help.
- Teach your children how to care for their home as they become old enough to handle the responsibilities. Take the time to train them how to do each job—they can't be expected to know unless they have been taught. Training them takes an investment of your time, but the investment will pay great dividends later on!
- Divide housecleaning into four jobs: kitchen, dusting, floors (mopping and vacuuming), and bathrooms. Then tackle just one job at a time.

Laundry

- Teach your children to sort laundry at an early age. Austin, who's four, helps me sort laundry several times each week.

- Come up with a plan of what works best for you, doing one or two loads each day, or doing laundry once a week.
- Pray for each person as you fold his or her clothing.
- Put away the clothes as soon as they are folded (or better yet, ask the owner of each pile to take them to his room and put them away!). This keeps the clothes in their home and not in piles in the living room, the laundry room, or in a laundry basket.
- If a load is left in the dryer and wrinkles have set in, spritz the load with a spray bottle of water, and dry for 10–15 minutes. Most wrinkles will come right out.
- Teach your children how to do laundry and then require their assistance when they are available. This will be invaluable training for their college years.
- Teach your children how to fold clothes, then let them practice as often as possible.

Simplify, Simplify, Simplify

- Regularly clean out drawers and throw or give things away. The less you have to manage, the easier it is to keep clean and organized.
- Give your children trash bags and have them clean out their rooms regularly. Give prizes for the most improvement!
- Use your time creatively. You can clean out one or two drawers (in the bedroom, kitchen, or bathroom) as you talk on the phone.
- If you save items for a garage sale, store them out of the living area of the house—this will keep you (and the kids) from retrieving them on impulse.
- If you don't save items for a garage sale, get them out of the house as soon as possible. Either trash them or keep a box (perhaps in the trunk of your car, ready to drop off) that you regularly take to the local mission or Goodwill store.
- If you don't wear it, get rid of it.
- If the kids don't wear it, get rid of it—no matter how cute it is or who gave it to them! Kids have their opinions about clothes (especially as they get older!), so allow for their preferences

and get clothes out of their drawers and closets that they won't wear.

PUT MOTHERING BEFORE HOUSEKEEPING

This chapter focused on the practical side of keeping a home. But remember your professional objective: to create a healthy, enjoyable, nurturing environment in which family relationships can thrive. If you become too busy to read your child a book because you must have a perfect house, you've lost your proper focus. If you become angry because your child did not fold the shirts correctly, you've focused on perfection rather than teaching and training. If you have such a desire for organization and cleanliness that you don't allow for playing with Play-Doh every once in a while, you've taken housekeeping to the extreme. As you manage your home, remember the difference between being organized and being fanatical. And seize the moments to teach the skills of housekeeping to your children to take into adulthood.

Do you remember what my friend Holly said about housekeeping? Anyone can keep a house, but not everyone bothers to make a home. As you consider your career training and development, blend the relational priorities with the housekeeping skills to make a home that exudes love and comfort to all who enter it.

——————— A STEP FURTHER. . . ———————

If you struggle with clutter, take a few minutes to identify some of the items in your house that do not have a home. As you create a home for each type of item, share this information with other family members.

֍

What financial goals do you have that might be met if spending was more regulated with a budget?

What goals do you have for the practical skills of house-keeping?

ᕲᕱ

What goals do you have for the relational skills of home-making?

chapter 16

BUILD AN INCREDIBLE RESUMÉ!

IT WAS TWO WEEKS BEFORE MY COLLEGE GRADUATION AND THE KITCHEN table was cluttered with papers. A grade transcript, a list of work experiences, several awards, and certificates were scattered in front of me. My goal was to pull it all together, put it on paper, and present my qualifications for employment. I was building my resumé.

The compilation of personal information, work and volunteer experience, a listing of accomplishments, topped off with a few character references: These are the makings of a good resumé. It is designed to be a document that briefly, yet specifically, shows the applicant's abilities, talents, training, and experience. As we take seriously the profession of motherhood we are using management and organizational skills. We become relationship specialists. Our ability to set vision and goals blended with our tenacity to stick with a job spell commitment. The years spent in the profession of motherhood allow a woman to build an incredible resumé!

AN ADJUSTMENT IN PERSPECTIVE

I started this book with a challenge to rethink the years spent mothering children. The term "profession" has been used throughout the chapters. After the children leave home we have two choices: to remain in the same line of work or to change careers. When we do make the shift to the next season we must, however, keep the perspective that motherhood is a valid profession. We must present ourselves as the professionals that we are in order for society to begin to change its view about full-time motherhood.

Most of us reading this book are not thinking much about the next season of our life. We're in the midst of sticky kitchen floors, piles of laundry, and never-ending carpool schedules. The only time I think much about the empty nest is when I'm daydreaming about really having a few moments to myself. Then I wake up and reality faces me once again.

It doesn't hurt us, though, to begin thinking about what our goals will be when we make the transition to the next season of life. What are our options? What do we want to do? What experience will we bring to that season of our lives?

Once again, we have choices. We may choose to reenter the paid workforce. We may return to school. Some of us may determine to remain at home taking seriously the job of homemaker, grandparent, neighbor, and friend. So many opportunities lie ahead of us!

IT'S NOT JUST A JOB, IT'S AN ADVENTURE!

If we choose to reenter the paid workforce we will take one of two routes. For some of us, it will be returning to our previous profession. The years spent investing in the lives of our family enrich our experience and allow us much wisdom and perspective as we return to our former careers. Updating our license, taking a few classes to refresh our knowledge, and adjusting to the concept of work hours may be necessary.

Others of us may never have had a career before we began the profession of motherhood. Motherhood is all we know. Or we may have worked in one profession, but desire to explore other options. The profession of motherhood has provided us with a variety of work experiences. Cindy Hays, a former bookstore owner, shared that when hiring employees she often experienced wonderful results when she hired a woman who had been committed to motherhood. "In my experience as an employer, mothers are women who have excellent management skills and good organizational abilities. They are responsible, reliable employees," stated Cindy.

Going back to school may also be an option for some of us. Dr. Brenda Hunter, a favorite speaker at Hearts at Home, returned to college to pursue her doctorate when her daughters were in their late teens. She has authored several books. She has made an impact on many lives as a psychotherapist, author, and speaker. It all happened after she raised her family.

Phyllis Schlafly, a mother of six, founded the Eagle Forum, a national, conservative political organization, at age fifty-one. For more than twenty years she has been a voice on Capitol Hill for traditional values. Many women pursue satisfying careers when they return to the paid workforce. It is possible to have several careers in a lifetime!

REMAINING AT HOME

Another option after the children leave the nest is to remain at home. The time formerly spent raising children can now be spent investing in other relationships. Our society desperately needs mentors and caregivers who can share their experience and love with others. As distance separates more and more extended families, the need for women to "mother the mother" only increases. Volunteers are desperately needed in schools, churches, and nonprofit organizations. The value of being an available grandparent cannot be underestimated. Even being a neighbor and a friend who has time to give to others is seriously needed in our fast-paced world.

After our children leave the home we can continue to stay home. It is a valid option. People need other people in their lives who have time to care and time to give. Your experience is a valuable asset to be shared with others.

PRESENTING OUR EXPERIENCE

One of the most important things we can do as we consider our life beyond motherhood is to keep the value of the profession in the forefront of our minds. A season of life spent in the career of motherhood is a season rich in experience. It is a time of life that both physical and intellectual energies are used to the fullest. We are developing an impressive resumé of knowledge and experience.

If we do reenter the paid workforce, we should never apologize for our years spent in the career of motherhood. Do not discount the years spent leading your son's Boy Scout troop. You garnered valuable conflict-resolution skills along with great resourcefulness. Don't forget about the years you committed to helping first graders read at your children's school. Your experience teaching literacy will be an asset to whatever you do. Maybe you are home schooling your children. What a resumé booster that is as you operate as a teacher, a manager, and a motivator of children! As a mom, you've become an experienced caregiver. Caregivers for both children and the ill and aged are in great demand. Years given to the profession of motherhood are years very well spent!

THE PROFESSION OF MOTHERHOOD

The profession of motherhood is indeed one of the most influential professions available to women. We are not only affecting the lives of our children but also our grandchildren, our great-grandchildren, and the generations to come. What we do today will affect the lives of those who follow us.

As we look to a new definition of accomplishment, we must focus on the long-term goals rather than the short-term projects.

As we understand our worth in Christ, we find our value.

As we learn to take care of ourselves, we discover balance in the daily demands of motherhood.

As we build a family that is marriage-centered, we provide our children with the stability they need.

As we realize the importance of building a community of mothers, we invest in each other's lives.

As we incorporate the tools of the trade into our lives, we find ourselves more equipped for the job.

As we grow our friendship with God, we set the cornerstone for our career training and development.

As we take our parenting responsibilities seriously, we move forward in teaching our children.

As we care for the physical and sometimes mundane chores of running a home, we find joy in providing a haven for our family.

Through it all, we are building a lifetime of invaluable experience—experience that can be taken into the paid workforce or experience that can continue to be used at home.

Have you captured the vision and value of keeping our hearts at home? There is no better job than one that invests in the lives of people. The profession of motherhood is a worthy profession. I wouldn't want to do anything else!

A Message for the Husband of a Woman in the Profession of Motherhood

HEARTS AT HOME IS AN ORGANIZATION DEDICATED TO ENCOURAGING and equipping women who take the job of wife and mother seriously. Most of our communication is directly with women in the profession of motherhood. Occasionally, though, we get the opportunity to share with their husbands.

I hope your wife has enjoyed reading this book. My prayer is that it instilled vision, provided encouragement, and helped equip her for one of the most important jobs in the world. Our organization provides a variety of resources to encourage your wife, but nothing will mean more than the encouragement she can receive from you. Many husbands don't know where to begin in communicating appreciation. Below is a letter our organization received. Maybe it will assist you in better understanding the unique job to which your wife is committed and the unique needs she has.

Dear Hearts at Home,

My wife is a full-time wife and mother. She does a wonderful job creating a warm, inviting home and handling all the responsibilities it takes to manage our family. Sometimes, though, I think she feels that I don't appreciate her. Any suggestions on how I can let her know that I do appreciate her?
—Scott

Dear Scott,

I'm so glad you asked! I only wish more husbands would ask that question. Here are a few thoughts to help you communicate and express your appreciation.

1. *Make sure you tell her.* Give her a hug after dinner and tell her how much you appreciated her work. The next time you find your laundry finished, thank her for taking care of that mundane chore. When the house is cleaned, tell her how great it looks. In other words, regularly comment on the work she does that most people take for granted (meals, cleaning, laundry, etc.). Even when she's had a bad day full of demanding children or unfinished chores, remind her of the value of the profession of motherhood. Tell her how much you appreciate her commitment to the family.

2. *Give her a bonus.* Homemakers don't make any money, of course, but you can still give her something extra. Maybe you could give her some time. Just a simple, "I'm taking the kids to the park. I'd like you to have an hour to yourself—you deserve it," can make all the difference in the world.

3. *Communicate to her that you value her presence at home.* Tell her how much you appreciate her commitment to making your home a place of warmth and encouragement. Thank her for her work teaching and training the children and being available to them. Help her keep perspective about the short season children are home and the value of capitalizing on that time in their lives.

4. *Discuss her needs for adult interaction and assist her in achieving some goals.* A mother at home with small children can find great benefit in having one evening out a week for herself. The rejuvenation that occurs from spending that time alone or with a friend can go a long way in helping her keep her individualism during a season that often saps identity and energy.

5. *Assist her in household tasks when you are home.* This brings a teamwork approach to the home and keeps responsibilities from feeling unbalanced.

6. *Talk, talk, talk to her!* Tell her about your day and ask her about hers. Listen with your eyes, look at her. Your communication with her will fill her emotional fuel tank.

7. *Take her out regularly.* A weekly or biweekly date says, "You are important to me. Our relationship is important." A getaway once a year goes a long way, too.

8. *Send her to a Hearts at Home conference and/or subscribe to the* Hearts at Home *magazine or devotional.* The conferences provide her with continuing education in her profession. The publications are her professional journals. These resources will greatly encourage her in the job she is doing.

When working in the paid workforce, one finds enjoyment in the job in direct proportion to the sense of accomplishment, the status of the relationship with coworkers, the pay, and the benefits. Working at home is no different. When it comes to a sense of accomplishment, you learn to adjust your expectations and look down the road twenty years for your evaluation of accomplishment. Instead of a regular paycheck, you receive pay in hugs, kisses, and snuggles on the couch. Instead of financial benefits, you have relational benefits. And instead of coworkers, you have one business partner—a husband—whose support and encouragement mean the world to you!

Keeping hearts at home,

Jill Savage

Founder and Director

MY PROFESSIONAL GOALS

Now that you have a better picture of the profession of motherhood, take some time to set some professional goals for yourself. With your mission statement and priority list in hand from page 54, begin to set goals for your relationship with God, your physical and emotional needs, your marriage, and your children. Below is an outline, but you may want to do this on your computer or on a separate sheet of paper.

If you've never taken time to set professional goals, this may take some time. It is time well spent, though, as goals are helpful in providing the target we are aiming towards. Without goals, we often wander aimlessly from one urgent need to another. We are reactive rather than proactive in our relationships. A mission statement and accompanying goals help us stay focused on our vision and maintain balance in our lives.

Start with prayer, asking God to help you clarify your thoughts. Revisit and revise your goals regularly. Our lives are changing all the time and our goals will need to reflect those changes.

Keep your goals where you can see them easily. Put them in your planner, post them on the bulletin board, or keep them in your Bible. Refer to them often to help you keep your vision fresh and your mind sharp.

<u>My Spiritual Goals</u> (refer to chapters 4 and 13)
Lifetime Goals

Annual Goals

Monthly Goals

Daily Goals

<u>My Personal Goals (Physical and Emotional)</u> (refer to chapters 1–3, 6, 7–12, 16)
Lifetime Goals

Annual Goals

Monthly Goals

Daily Goals

<u>My Marriage Goals</u> (refer to chapters 5 and 7)
Lifetime Goals

Annual Goals

Monthly Goals

Daily Goals

<u>My Parenting Goals</u> (refer to chapters 7–11, 14)
Lifetime Goals

Annual Goals

Monthly Goals

Daily Goals

(You can also break parenting goals into separate
goals you have for each child.)

PROFESSIONAL RESOURCES FOR MOTHERS AT HOME

Hearts at Home Conferences and Resources
Hearts at Home Magazine
Hearts at Home Devotional
309–888–MOMS; www.hearts-at-home.org, 900 W. College Ave., Normal, IL 61761

OTHER ORGANIZATIONS FOR MOTHERS

Mothers of Preschoolers (MOPS), 303–733–5353
National Association of At-Home Mothers, 405 E. Buchanan Ave., Fairfield, IA, 52556
MOCAH (Mothers of Color At Home), PO Box 188, Union City, GA, 30291
Mothers At Home, 1–800–783–4MOM

ADDITIONAL RECOMMENDED RESOURCES LISTED BY TOPIC

Developing a Friendship with God

Come Walk With Me by Carole Mayhall
Too Busy Not To Pray by Bill Hybels

When Mother's Pray by Cheri Fuller
Let Prayer Change Your Life by Becky Tirabassi
Moms In Touch, International, 619–486–4065
Focus on the Family, 1–800–A–FAMILY

Friendships

The Friendships of Women by Dee Brestin

Grace

Families Where Grace Is in Place by Jeff VanVonderen

Homemaking

The Messies Manual by Sandra Felton
Home Comfort by Cheryl Mendelson

Marriage

Intimate Issues by Linda Dillow and Loraine Pintus
His Needs, Her Needs by Willard Harley
The Power of a Praying Wife by Stormie Omartian
A Celebration of Sex by Dr. Douglas E. Rosanau
Marriage Partnership Magazine, 1–800–628–4942
Family Life Marriage Seminars, 1–800–333–1433

Motherhood

Don't Miss Your Kids by Charlene Baumbich
Women Leaving the Workspace by Larry Burkett
A Mother's Heart by Jean Fleming
So You Want to Be a Stay at Home Mom by Cheryl Gochnauer
Home by Choice by Dr. Brenda Hunter
What Every Mom Needs by Elisa Morgan and Carol Kuykendall
The Power of a Praying Parent by Stormie Omartian
The Stay-at-Home Mom by Donna Otto

NOTES

1. U.S. Bureau of Labor Statistics, Department of Labor, *Current Population Survey 1998*, excerpted from unpublished marital and family tables, Table 8, collected by U.S. Census Bureau (Washington, D.C., 1998).

2. Dr. Brenda Hunter, *Home by Choice* (Sisters, OR: Multnomah 2000).

3. Jean Fleming, *A Mother's Heart* (Colorado Springs, CO: NavPress 1990), 120.

4. Elise Arndt, *A Mother's Time.*

5. Linda Weber, *Mom, You're Incredible!* (Colorado Springs, CO: Focus on the Family, 1994), 157–158.

6. Ibid.

7. Arndt, *A Mother's Time.*

8. Stormie Omartian, *The Power of a Praying Parent* (Eugene, OR: Harvest House, 1995).

9. Fleming, *A Mother's Heart.*

10. Jeff VanVonderen, *Families Where Grace Is in Place* (Minneapolis, MN: Bethany House, 1992), 139–140. Adapted and used with permission.

11. Ibid., 15.

12. Ibid., 140–46.

13. Ibid., 26.

14. The Hope Health Letter of The Hope Heart Institute.

15. David Burke, "Children Are Anarchists," *Hearts at Home*, vol. 2, no. 9 (September 2000), 10–11.

Hearts at Home

The Hearts at Home organization is committed to meeting the needs of women in the profession of motherhood. Founded in 1993, Hearts at Home offers a variety of resources and events to assist women in their jobs as wives and mothers.

Find out how Hearts at Home can provide you with ongoing education and encouragement in the profession of motherhood. In addition to this book, our resources include the *Hearts at Home* magazine, the *Hearts at Home* devotional, and our Hearts at Home website. Additionally, Hearts at Home events make a great getaway for individuals, moms' groups, or for that special friend, sister, or sister-in-law. The regional conferences, attended by over ten thousand women each year, provide a unique, affordable, and highly encouraging weekend for the woman who takes the profession of motherhood seriously.

Hearts at Home
900 W. College Avenue
Normal, Illinois 61761
Phone: (309) 888-MOMS
Fax: (309) 888-4525
E-mail: hearts@dave-world.net
Web: www.hearts-at-home.org